LANGUAGE LEARNER GUIDEBOOK

POWERFUL TOOLS TO HELP YOU CONQUER ANY LANGUAGE

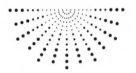

SHANE DIXON

WAYZGOOSE PRESS

ISBN 978-1-938757-46-4

CONTENTS

FOREWORD

BY DR. JUSTIN SHEWELL

One of my most memorable experiences in working with Dr. Shane Dixon was filming a video for one of the courses in our award-winning online TESOL certificate program, *Teach English Now!* Imagine if you will, Shane, covered in blue body paint from waist to head, wearing a turban and playing the role of the genie of the lamp to help teachers learn how to teach the writing process! That is an example of the lengths Shane will go to help his learners understand and remember important concepts. He has a way of taking the most important concepts and combining them with just the right metaphors to help them stick in his learners' memories and transfer into real-life application.

I am honored to have been asked to write this foreword for the *Language Learner Guidebook* because I believe in its concepts. I have used many of these techniques myself to learn the Korean language and Korean Sign Language, and have encouraged many of my learners to use them to improve their learning of English.

I also believe in Shane as a language teacher, or "language

guide," if you will. I first met Shane 14 years ago, when we were both teaching English as a Second Language part-time at the English Language Center at Brigham Young University in Provo, Utah. Later, when I came to Arizona State University after spending six years teaching at the United Arab Emirates University, I interviewed for a job at the American English and Culture Program and was surprised to run into Shane again.

Since then we have worked together on a variety of projects, including co-designing the world's largest online TESOL certificate program. Our unique way of incorporating metaphors and narratives into our educational videos led to our course winning the first-ever "Learners First Award" from Coursera in 2016, beating out over 1,800 other courses, and catching the attention of notable education expert Dr. Barbara Oakley, who collaborated with us on our latest course, *Learning How to Learn a Language*, the companion course to this book!

The *Language Learner Guidebook* will help you understand some of the most fundamental concepts in language learning, starting with the idea that language learning doesn't happen in a classroom! This *Guidebook* will help you answer five questions that every language learner should ask themselves, and create a community of resources around you.

It will help you make effective use of even those small moments by engaging in short language learning adventures and getting more out of your language learning activities.

You'll learn how to avoid two common pitfalls that trap many language learners, and how to establish a language learning ecosystem that will keep your language learning efforts alive long after the novelty has worn off.

You'll learn how to look inside yourself and reflect on your language learning successes and failures, and how to keep yourself motivated even when it seems you are not making any progress in your language learning journey.

Most importantly, you'll have fun doing it! You'll laugh; you'll cry; you'll be pulled in and may not even realize you're learning as you go. That is the magic of Shane's "sneaky" teaching methods.

Let the adventures begin!

Justin Shewell

PART I
THE FIVE QUESTIONS YOU NEED TO ASK YOURSELF

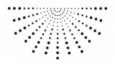

What if I told you that with five simple questions, I can determine whether you will learn a language? It is not a trick—it is experience.

That experience began in Baghdad.

THE VERY FIRST THING YOU NEED

THERE IS A STRANGE SORT OF BEAUTY TO BAGHDAD IN A DUST storm. The sky turns a reddish orange, and the wind whips the palm tree fronds into a frenzied quiver reminiscent of small children waving frantically. Strange is the right word for how I felt as I witnessed my first Iraqi dust storm.

It was the summer of 2010, and I was thousands of miles from home. At that very moment, I found myself just outside the Al Rasheed hotel, looking up to notice not only the orange color that painted the sky, but also that the hotel was recently pockmarked by mortar fire. My colleagues and I shielded our faces from the sand as we walked inside the hotel, where hotel patrons escorted us to a second-floor terrace and then a banquet room. This immense room with tall ceilings would serve as our classroom, and here, over the course of two months, we would train nearly two hundred Iraqi nationals to become English teacher trainers.

The U.S. Department of State had sent me and four other Arizona State University instructors to stay in a militarized zone, leaving our compound each day—the occasional dust storms notwithstanding—to teach at the hotel. The Green Zone, as it was popularly known, was four square miles replete with concrete blast walls, security checkpoints, two military bases, and the largest U.S. Embassy in the world.

Military personnel and private security firms looked right at home in the zone, as armored vehicles rumbled and soldiers with automatic weapons stood at attention. I, on the other hand, most certainly looked out of place. Rather than a gun, I had my beat-up acoustic guitar slung across my back, and in either hand, I held suitcases full of teacher supplies. If anyone had needed me to provide a gun, he or she would have been out of luck—but glue sticks? I had three.

This was a shocking turn of events for someone like me.

Let me explain. I am—or was—just an English teacher in the U.S. I taught English to international students, mostly those interested in attending an American university. My career had kept me mostly inside the U.S., and adventure had never been my strong suit. My students, on the other hand, came from all over the world, giving up their home lives seeking all kinds of dreams. While they all had and have a similar end goal—a university degree—there is a great variety in what they believe they can achieve with that degree. Some wish to return home to support a family business, while others wish to fundamentally change society, politics, or law. Others wish to create new business models or push the technological envelope. In the end, this boils down to a single desire: they all wish to be amazing. I love this about my students. I love what they aspire to become. For me, as an educator, amazing is always the right goal.

However, when the opportunity arose to do something amazing myself, I flinched a bit. Amazing is what my students do, not me. Yet something nagged at me, a truth that I buried deep inside my gut in hopes it would go away. It did not, and eventually I had to confront it head on. The truth was this: if I was constantly asking my students to leave their countries, open their mouths, try foods they had never tried, and be in difficult circumstances away from their home, I would sound false if I was not willing to risk myself.

Risk, as I had preached repeatedly to my students, is the most basic of language principles, and, as you might have guessed already, by being willing to risk myself, the unexpected occurred. For it was here that I was first introduced to the five questions that would help me learn and/or improve a second, third, and—coming soon—a fourth language. Like many realizations, however, it began with a first step and a key takeaway. The takeaway, you might say, looked like this:

Learning a language requires risk.
Risk puts you in contact with amazing.
Amazing is always the right goal.

2

WAFA'A

Iraq was amazing.

One of the first people I met was Wafa'a: dark skinned, bright-eyed, and shawled in the Muslim fashion. It was impossible to miss her: she always sat in the front row, and in every class, she sat down with an open notebook and pen in hand. She was a young teacher trainer from Basra, a city in the southern part of Iraq, and when I inquired what it was like at schools in her city, she showed me a picture of a school without a roof.

"What do you do when it rains?" I asked.

She smiled demurely. I noticed that sometimes among the Arabic female teachers, a question was not always met with a straight answer, and I had learned to accept that fact. She showed me other pictures of young learners crammed into desks, some in the back of the classroom either standing or sitting on the floor, with no desks or chairs at all. There was a remarkable amount of smiling in these pictures, which melted my heart.

"Twenty-five minutes for each class. Administrators tell us to give announcements for five minutes, and then explain an assignment for ten. This gives students the remaining ten minutes of class. Only ten minutes to actually practice!"

Her exasperation was something I would hear repeatedly. Over the course of two months, I heard dozens of stories like Wafa'a's. They spoke of a lack of time, resources, and trained instructors. The stories fascinated and concerned me, so I attempted to gather as many of them as I could.

First, I tried to find out administrative difficulties, things that handcuffed the teachers so that they could not do their job. I noticed that administrator buy in was rare, and in the best of scenarios, learners were exposed to only five hours of English a week, with much of that time taken by administrative announcements and managing bad classroom behavior.

I also gathered as much information as I could about what the teachers were doing in the classroom such as the curriculum and strategies they employed, either by choice or by mandate.

Finally, I wanted to know how they learned language; how did these two hundred teacher trainers become so amazing themselves? What had they done to learn English, a language that is not spoken in the streets, in the homes, or in the daily lives of a typical Iraqi?

Learning their stories caused me a lot of reflection and allowed me to come to my first major conclusion. I must admit it was a disturbing one, and one that I felt compelled to test and retest over the next few years by speaking with hundreds of other teachers in similar training programs. My conclusion was this: very few, if any, of the teachers I interviewed believed that they learned English in a classroom. In fact, most of them stated flatly that language learning only happened when they stepped beyond the classroom doors.

During training, I felt compelled to share my insights with the Iraqi teachers, helping them confront the fact that they themselves were learning in a way that was out of harmony with their own instructional practices. The revelation reverberated among the group, and changed the direction of my training. I created metaphors and principles based on what we were learning, and asked teachers to do the same.

Another day of training, and Wafa'a was in the front row again, notebook neatly in her lap. With a pen in hand and a furrowed brow, she listened until something captured her. Then, when a thought would strike, her eyes would light up with excitement like someone on a diving expedition who had just caught a pearl. She would return feverishly to her notebook, as if afraid her idea would slip away if her pen strokes were not fast enough. I myself spent nights scribbling as well, hoping that my discussions with this group would lead me to my own string of pearls. The first one, I knew, I had already found. It looked something like this:

Language is not, and has never been, learned in a classroom.

That revelation led me to the very first of my five questions:

Question 1: Am I willing to go outside the classroom?

3

OUTSIDE THE LINES: THE LANGUAGE LEARNING ECOSYSTEM

Q: So how did those Iraqi teachers you met in 2010 learn English?
A: The same way teachers and students from Peru, Mexico, China, and Jordan are learning languages right now.

OVER THE NEXT FEW YEARS, AND HUNDREDS OF INTERVIEWS later, I came to a startling discovery: language learning is happening even in the remote jungles of Peru, the Sierra Madre mountain ranges in southeast Mexico, and the western edge of the Sichuan Basin. Even in Syrian refugee camps, language can and is happening…and not only is it happening, but in a way that the world has never seen before.

After returning from Baghdad to my home in Arizona, I have continued training teachers. These groups can come from just about anywhere in the world, and, if the cards fall just right, they receive funding to come to the U.S. and experience American culture (and education) firsthand.

In 2015, it was a young group of 195 Mexican teachers. Early on a Monday morning, they stood in line ready to receive

ID cards, vaccinations, and textbooks. I was selected to lead the program as the educational director, and so I was there in suit and tie to represent ASU as best I could.

While I find it important to have them get to know what Arizona State is all about, I find it equally important to get to know each of these Mexican teachers, and so I go down the line trying to learn names. I have a memory trick that I use to remember as many as possible.

"What's your name?" I ask.

"Julio Cesar," the first teacher says.

"Do you know Julio Cesar Chavez?" I ask.

"The fighter?" he replies with his own question and throws me a jab. I like Julio Cesar. He is immediately friendly.

"That's right. My dad loves boxing. If I forget your name, will you remind me by throwing that punch?" He agrees and pretends to punch again. Julio Cesar, I think to myself. Julio Cesar. The fighter. I imagine him in a ring and I am the announcer. The image makes me smile.

"So, how did you learn English?"

He tells me that he grew up listening to the radio, and that he loves heavy metal. He shares some of his favorite songs. He also mentions *Game of Thrones* and *Prison Break*. Down the line, I hear murmurs of agreement.

"I love *Prison Break*, but not as much as *Breaking Bad*."

This declaration surprises me. I have not seen either of these shows. As they continue to share, I get the distinct feeling that this group understands American pop culture in ways that I do not.

"I watch *Friends*," one older teacher says.

"Friends? You watch your friends?" says her companion.

"No, it's a TV show, *tonta*. Just like your *Game of Thrones*."

"I watch YouTube videos."

"I read the *New York Times*."

"I love to play games online with English-speaking friends."

"I listen to podcasts."

"Podcasts? No one listens to podcasts, you nerd. I love the Lakers. I watch all their games."

I go down the line and continue to memorize names. I meet Diana and think of the Roman goddess of the same name, goddess of the hunt. I ask Diana to pull back an invisible bow and shoot an invisible arrow. She agrees.

I meet Magalys, who shares the name of a Venezuelan friend of mine, a singer. After some discussion, we agree that she will clasp her hands together as if ready to sing opera. Her eyebrows rise comically and I almost expect her to belt out a song. I will not be able to forget her now—that is for sure.

As I continue farther and farther down the line, I keep learning and asking questions, trying to remember not only names and faces, but understanding what each teacher is currently doing to support their language learning.

Can you guess what the next lesson I learned was? While I witnessed this first in Iraq, these follow up trainings were instructive. No matter if I were with people from Mexico, Peru, or China, people are beginning to learn language without ever leaving their country. This, I thought, was something new. This is something worth trying to understand in full. Here are the key takeaways:

- There is a shift in how people are learning languages.
- Languages are learned by tapping into, and creating, vibrant, often-virtual communities.
- Anyone can do it.

While I will write about this in more detail later, I have learned that successful adult learners systematically search for authentic materials and relationships, and because of the explosion of available resources in the virtual world, this kind of approach can happen just about anywhere.

I refer to this approach as the successful learner's "language ecosystem." Here is the hopelessly academic definition: A language ecosystem describes a holistic environment that encourages and extends the learning and application of language beyond the classroom through a diverse system of tasks and incentives.

Now let me explain without all the fancy talk: developing an ecosystem means stepping out of the classroom, making a plan, and above all, exploring.

As soon as you see what I mean in the chapters ahead, you will find language learning is unbelievably fun.

Question 2: Am I willing to explore, online and in my own community?

3.5 NOT EVEN A CHAPTER, JUST A SLIGHT DETOUR

You may doubt that everyone can connect to virtual resources such as streaming music, movies, and videos. After all, there are people who do not even have access to the Internet, right? Yes, absolutely.

I am not suggesting that Internet access is equal everywhere, nor is every language equally represented on the Internet. You would be correct in assuming that some will be limited in their quest to create a virtual community in the language of their choice. All that said; let me counter this line of thinking, at least a bit, by telling you about my trip to Jordan.

It is now December of 2017, and I am riding alongside my fellow ASU compatriot, Nick. We are in an SUV rumbling through a Syrian refugee camp. We enter a city-sized expanse filled with thousands of colorful, hastily constructed concrete structures, not much larger than tents. These constructions, called caravans, are where each family lives. Some are a drab white, but many are painted. I saw SpongeBob Squarepants painted on the entire side of one caravan, and an Arabic phrase gracefully painted on another.

This kind of incongruity I see throughout the camp. Two women are dressed in traditional full-length hijabs, for example, but the man behind them is wearing a Golden State Warriors t-shirt. A man in a robe encourages a donkey to pull a cart, yet right past him are young boys with smartphones huddled near a fence looking for better cell reception.

"Wait...they have cellphones?"

"Yes," Raed, our guide and a camp director, explains, "they are all looking for service. We only have two cell towers in Za'atari camp."

"You have *two* towers? What do they look for on their cellphones?" I ask.

"Anything they can."

Cellphones in a refugee camp! I think about my own efforts to bring English to these camps, about ASU's own English courses and how mobile-friendly they are becoming. I think of possible interactions through Skype or Google Hangouts. I think of the other institutions and non-profits here in the camp: the Norwegian and Dutch Refugee Councils, and wonder if they will begin teaching in Norwegian or Dutch. I see now that the future is broader than I had expected, even for those living in temporary shelters like those that I see here. Even in a makeshift Syrian refugee camp, young learners are connecting, and no one can stop them.

People want connections, and they are bound to find them.

Want to read more about my experience in Jordan? Check out my blog: http://askmrlanguageperson.blogspot.com/

4

ROSETTA STONE IS A BOWFLEX

As a so-called language-learning expert, often I am asked about the effectiveness of some right-out-of-the-box commercial solution for language learning. The question goes something like this: "So, what do you think of Rosetta Stone/Duolingo/Busuu/OtherGenericOnlineProduct?"

My answer: Rosetta Stone is a Bowflex. Let me return you to Iraq to explain. After an exhausting day of teacher training at the Al Rasheed hotel, my group and I went back through a security checkpoint to head to our compound. Security guards at the checkpoint were from South America and Africa, and often greeted us with friendly smiles, which felt slightly out of place given the stern-looking automatic weapons they held in front of them. A few of these guards, at least over the course of the training, opened up to us, and even asked us for tips on learning English.

One day, an African guard named Michael got my email address, and I received a message that very night.

"Rosetta Stone—good?" he asked.

I was unsure how to respond. It was not that I was against

these products. I thought then, and still believe now, that products like Rosetta Stone fill an important space in the market. They often come equipped with excellent visuals and smart, carefully constructed lessons that lead you from one language item to another.

Yet something nagged at me. Since I could not quite put my finger on it, I decided to go work out. I am something of a gym rat, and one of the few benefits at the security compound was the gym on the first floor, just around the corner from the dining area.

I descended the stairs, turned the corner, and walked into the gym, which boasted a number of machines and free weights, and even had a TV situated in the back corner. It was on—the Al Jazeera channel blaring. After some brief news reporting, a commercial break came on, and I was surprised to see a commercial for Bowflex.

If you are not familiar with Bowflex, perhaps the easiest way to describe it is this: it is a single multi-function exercise machine advertised as an alternative to gym use. The commercials tend to show men and women with bodies that are, well, let's say slightly better than mine, all working out with the Bowflex and smiling like they are on a ride at Disneyland. That is when it hits me.

While I believe the Bowflex can be a perfectly fine product that can give you a good work out, systems like Bowflex—you know, systems that tout a one-stop shop/complete and total solution—generally aren't total solutions at all. Let us be honest. The ads themselves are at least slightly deceptive; these people are not exclusively doing Bowflex. Not with those biceps. They are trainers and models who spend inordinate amounts of time doing a variety of deliberate, focused exercise.

On top of the obvious but forgivable overselling, there is the problem of use. What is the typical result for the person who buys a Bowflex? At the risk of offending the entire home gym industry, let me state that, in my personal experience, I have noticed that people who buy a Bowflex generally end up with a Bowflex. What I mean is that instead of huge gains in fitness, most consumers end up instead with a giant Bowflex in their living rooms or basements, often collecting dust and cluttering their homes (In fact, I can't find the study, but I heard once that scientists discovered these machines actually expand in size the less they are used).

After years of non-use, most people begrudgingly admit their mistake; put their good intentions up for sale, and hope someone else with grand ambitions (and at least a bit of delusion) comes along looking for a single solution to all his or her exercise needs.

In a similar fashion, many commercial language products such as Rosetta Stone also oversell and under-deliver. Again, this is not to say that I do not recommend or use these products. I sometimes do. However, what I am suggesting is that we should not believe the commercials. These commercial products tell you that they will give you the keys to language learning success, with images of their product in the hands of good-looking people with broad smiles (Disneyland!). These people appear to have outrageous success in short periods.

However, the truth is that for the great majority of learners who purchase such products, the thrill of the language learning is short lived, and the ability to progress is limited. I would learn this from personal experience just a short time after my email exchange with Michael.

Here is what happened. After I returned from Iraq, I served as the computer coordinator for our department at ASU, and managed all our software solutions. It was during this time that a Rosetta Stone sales representative with nice hair and great teeth by the name of Vance Overstreet (yes, that was his name) presented and then sold a software package to my ASU faculty. I was put in charge of administering the licenses, which would be given first come first serve.

The results? All thirty licenses were quickly spoken for, and the teachers expressed immediate excitement. However, just over a month later, I went onto the website as the administrator to see how everyone was doing. To my surprise, all thirty teachers except one had stopped completely.

When I dug deeper into the data, I discovered that of the twenty-nine dropouts, only two of them had gotten past the second week of instruction. When I pushed for teachers to share why they stopped, they generally could not tell me except to speak in bland terms that life got in the way. Rosetta Stone was metaphorically placed in each teacher's basement, collecting dust and causing no small amount of guilt among the faculty members.

Back to Michael. What was I supposed to tell him? Most people looking to learn a language want a simple, pithy answer. Sharing a single product does that for them. However, the more I thought about it, the more I felt that if I endorsed one single product, any single product, no matter how good, I was being dishonest. The truth is, people do not need a Bowflex; they need a gym.

Question 3: Am I willing to find a variety of resources and not rely on a single choice to learn a language?

LEARNING SMART, NOT HARD

SEE IF THIS PROBLEM SOUNDS FAMILIAR. A LANGUAGE LEARNER, Andy, works hard memorizing a vocabulary word or some other bit of language, just as a good student should. Then something happens. The next day he gets a chance to speak to someone—an actual conversation—but while trying to remember what he studied, it seems to have disappeared completely. Andy is embarrassed and frustrated to discover that something so recently studied just does not seem to stick.

It gets worse. Andy begins to think that this event is a sign that he is not good at learning language. He reasons to himself that he must have a bad memory or lack that special gift to speak a language. As a result, a short time later, he gives up thinking that learning a language is just not for him.

Do you relate? If this is not familiar to you at all, it is certainly familiar to me. I have met and interviewed hundreds of people like Andy, all with a similar story and conclusion: I just did not have what it takes.

False.

What these individuals fail to realize is that they are, barring a learning disorder or serious mental disability, just like everyone else. Language is not something you learn just to score high on a test. In fact, learning a language is not like learning math or science—it is, well, slippery. Since language is slippery (I will explain the science more later), rather than studying it like any other discipline, think of it more like basketball. Again, language is not like math or science; language is basketball. Here is a fictitious story to help you see why.

Imagine Michael Jordan is teaching a basketball class. Do you think it would be well attended? Of course! It is Michael Jordan. Now imagine that he tells everyone he has written "the book" on basketball: *How to Play Basketball,* by Michael Jordan. Now imagine that he has written a dozen chapters, and that all the chapters together contain every concept and rule of basketball. There are chapters on dribbling, passing, shooting, and, of course, dunking. He further explains that every Friday he will have a test so that he can ensure that students have learned all the information.

Imagine once more that the students, loving Michael Jordan the way they do, all studiously memorize the book, prepare for every test, and, in fact, get perfect scores. On the last day of the class, Michael Jordan puts a basketball in front of the class and states, "Students—I am so proud of you. You read my book. You know all the rules. You have passed every test. Now you can play basketball like Michael Jordan!"

How much would you agree with that last statement? My guess is that most of you would very strongly disagree. Now think about why you feel this way. A word, in fact, may have popped into your mind without me supplying it for you. The word is practice.

Language is basketball is a phrase I use to remind learners of the necessity not only to study, memorize, and learn language, but also to put that language into action. One of my mentors,

Mark Rentz, used the mantra *Learn a little; use it a lot* to express much the same idea.

Let us go back to our poor struggling learner, Andy. He studied, he memorized, and he could probably even take a test and prove that he knows words on a list. He knows rules, and he has absorbed a lot of information, but he is not able to recall them during the flow of the conversation. In other words, he has learned a language, but he cannot use it automatically. To go back to our analogy, he has studied a lot about basketball, but that is very different from playing basketball.

The more you realize that language is a game that you play, a system that you put into action, the more you will understand why so many fail to learn. To speak frankly, most study hard without studying right. Another way to say this is that people focus too much on receiving information about a language without trying out that information. As you consider your own language plan, please remember that while studying is very important, without practice, you will never be successful. Practice is key.

Question 4: Am I willing to practice what I learn about my target language right away?

MAKING AND KEEPING FRIENDSHIPS

So what languages do I know? This question always makes me just a bit uncomfortable. Let me tell you why. I speak English, Spanish, Portuguese, a little French, and I am dabbling in a few others. If I'm cornered, I might say, perhaps, three and a half languages. I would say it, but I would be a bit uncomfortable saying it.

The reason for my discomfort is that language learning is such a slow, piece-by-piece process, and it is hard to tell when someone has finally 'arrived.' In fact, the idea itself, this idea of 'arriving' in language, is flawed. Language, you see, is more of a journey than a destination, and most learners never feel comfortable saying they have arrived when asked about how much they know. This is especially true because, as in all educational pursuits, the more you learn, the more you are aware of what you do not know.

To illustrate, many of my students are quite proficient in English. In fact, they are so proficient that they are just about ready to enter Arizona State University as freshman. However, even they squirm when people ask them if they speak English. Here are the answers I most often hear:

- *I speak okay.*
- *I'm not so good.*
- *I don't know.*

The truth is that even these excellent English speakers often feel the distance between them and native-like proficiency. They have accents, they do not know certain words (the word *squirm*, for example, would be hard for many of them), and they constantly second-guess their grammar. The question "Do you speak a language?" comes out sounding, in their ears, a lot like "Have you mastered the language?"

Contrast the feeling of uncertainty my students have with the feelings of their parents. Parents of my students are usually back at home showing pictures of their English-speaking son or daughter. Most of these parents beam with pride when asked about their son or daughter's English abilities. Almost without exception, students confess to me that their parents' reactions are more like this:

"My son? He's at ASU. He speaks perfect English."

"My daughter? She's so smart in English. She speaks so well, people don't even know she's from Taiwan."

So how can my students, who by all accounts are doing these amazing things in the United States, still feel like they have not arrived?

The truth is this: when we focus on mastering a language: perfect pronunciation, complete command of the vocabulary, ability to speak in any and every possible situation, we are always going to feel insufficient, because by that measure, we all fall short. This way of learning a language is exhausting.

It does not have to be that way. A better question than "Do

you know the language?" is this: "In the language you are learning, are you creating friendships and experiences?"

I know that is a very different question, but stay with me. What I am suggesting is that learners reframe their perspectives. Rather than thinking of language as a destination, it is much more productive and fruitful if we can think of language as a series of milestones in the road of life. Those milestones, more often than not, involve meeting people and having amazing experiences.

Let us go back to my students again. While my students are probably correct that their language is not as perfect as it could be (and in some cases, should be), what they are accomplishing is otherworldly. They are simply so close to the situation that they do not see themselves as amazing.

Parents, on the other hand, are not constantly faced with this kind of self-doubt, and in my view, actually see things from a far better perspective. Parents tend to focus on what their son or daughter is achieving, looking at their son or daughter's experience rather than perfection. My daughter is in the United States...and she is making it.

My point is that, as you begin or continue your language journey, when you are tempted to look at the top of the Language Mountain and think, *I will never get there*, take courage and remember that you are having an experience...and that you are making it. Furthermore, as you take inventory of what you are doing, I strongly believe that if it does not involve people and experiences, you will likely burn out. However, if you are fueled by meeting others, trying new things, and making memories and friendships for yourself, you have a great shot.

In the chapters that follow, I will introduce both my friends and experiences to you. This book is sentimental in part because of my belief that language learning is, at its core, about relationships and experiences—about connecting and learning from those connections. I hope that by telling stories and sharing my experiences, you will come to see exciting insights that will both motivate and direct your efforts.

I have already introduced you to Wafa'a and her attitude that good things can come just by believing. Soon I will introduce you to Nigar, with her fiery spirit and indomitable way of looking at life. You will meet Mariela, who did not let obstacles dictate her own life, and I will introduce you to others such as Daisy and Haru. It is my belief that every story (even those who fail) can teach us something about language learning.

Question 5: Am I willing to step outside of myself and make new friendships and experiences?

7

NATIONAL PLANS

ON A HOT MORNING IN THE SUMMER OF 2015, YOU WOULD have found me outside the oddly shaped Peruvian Ministry of Education (MINEDU) in Lima, Peru. Up close, each floor of this odd building looked slightly askew, as if children had stacked blocks with their eyes closed. From a distance, however, I could see the architect's intent: it looked like textbooks placed one on top of the other. In other words, the building was a symbol meant to remind officials of the purpose behind their office jobs. The building was in the shape of a stack of books to remind everyone that their job, ultimately, was to bring knowledge to students. Only by standing back, however, could I, or anyone, see the symbol—stacked books—clearly.

While I was contemplating this visual metaphor, an escort came out to greet me. I followed her into a boardroom, where I stood in front of a group of ministry officials dressed in grey suits. I admit I was nervous. I had been invited previously to share my views on a recent training conducted at ASU, as well as how the training might fit into the current success of the national plan. The problem was that, while I knew that the training at ASU was successful, I was certain (as were the 235 teachers) that the national plan was setting the teachers up to fail.

The national language plan, with its motto *Puertas Al Mundo* (Doors to the World), was ambitious and well-funded. This plan offered a robust multi-million dollar increase in spending for English teachers throughout Peru, as well as investments in technology and online training. Four thousand teachers were identified as potential instructors in carrying out this plan, and several university partners, including my own, were selected for training. The goal: by 2021, all graduating high school students would have high intermediate levels of English.

Sounds good so far, right? More money, better training, more teachers. These are all worthy goals.

However, knowing what you know already about my five questions, see if you can spot why I was certain failure would follow. The plan demonstrated a significant investment of dollars that went primarily to increased classroom instruction, (from three to five hours). The other large investment came in the form of a materials upgrade, specifically in the purchase of a single software solution (in this case, a software program produced by a British language company). Teachers would move lockstep with the curriculum, with the two additional hours going directly to time spent in front of a computer screen working only on the software solution. No significant investment in time or money was allocated for students to communicate with each other or with language partners.

Peru had been sold a Bowflex, and I knew it.

This was not the first time I had seen large government dollars go to a well-intentioned project. Let me share two other examples. The first happened while in Iraq, where I met the director of a language library that the U.S. government built. The library was, by this director's accounting, worth millions of dollars. He described the center as state of the art, with books and videos placed neatly on rows of shelves. However, the center was not intended for student use, and teachers had to travel after school to check out the materials. It was not a place to meet, greet, or interact.

"Dust!" he exclaimed, slamming a fist on the table. "The books just gather dust. No one uses this center, and it just collects dust."

One final example. A few years later ASU was asked to bid on a project based on the national language plan for Vietnam, and again, millions of dollars were at play. Our lead proposal writer for this project, Jimmy Cervin, headed to Vietnam to see what we could coordinate. While we were able to extend our influence to a few trainings in Ho Chi Minh City, Jimmy showed frustration at the unwillingness for the government to do more. The government, he said, was afraid to spend more money, citing that half of the money on the national plan was already spent on trainings and software solutions, with no significant increase in language ability.

Experiences like these deeply influenced what I wanted to share with the ministry of education in Peru. I breathed deeply, and started by sharing good news. Our recent training with hundreds of Peruvian public school English teachers was success-ful. It had revolved around the language ecosystem concept, meaning that teachers and learners were taught to think outside of the classroom and outside of a single product (in fact, in a single month we taught over 50 different technologies students can use to learn a language). We were confident that the Peruvian teachers now had technologies, incentives, and ideas to get students to create and connect. I shared with the ministry how excited teachers were to get back to their students and make a difference.

I then made a plea that, instead of a single software solution and an increase in class time, a wiser investment of dollars could go to the creation of these ecosystems. I envisioned teachers creating language camps, language clubs, online communities, and many other exciting possibilities. We envisioned that a few of the trained teachers could train others throughout Peru to help students create their own ecosystems. We wanted students to explore products, videos, and music on their own, and invite students to share what they found with the rest of their classmates. We wanted to help learners learn in the same fashion as their teachers. Through community. Through exploration. Through a plan.

Ready to see what a plan might look like for you? Read the free, downloadable resource, an individual language plan to help you begin getting basic ideas for your very own language ecosystem:

http://www.language-warriors.com/language-plan

Ready to learn even more? Then I invite you to meet Dr. Francois Gouin, who came to some of the same conclusions 150 years before I did, but did so in spectacular style.

QUESTIONS FOR GROUP DISCUSSION

1. Why do you think people fail to learn languages?
2. Do you know anyone who has succeeded in learning a language? How did he or she do it?
3. What excites you about learning a new language? What makes you nervous?
4. People plan difficult tasks such as building a house or running a marathon. Why do you think people fail to plan their language learning?

PART II
EXPLORE

Wanderers are not lost, they are looking.

8

HOW CAN IMMERSION FAIL?

A VERY COMMON PHRASE, AND ONE WITH WHICH I DO NOT entirely disagree, is this: "The best way to learn a language is immersion." Immersion, many believe, is the ONLY way to learn a language. To state the sentiment colloquially, you must throw yourself into the pool to swim! However, as much as I love the advantages that immersion can bring, I want to pose a question. Is it possible to be in another country—surrounded by people who speak that language—and still fail?

The answer is simple. Not only is it possible, but it is more common than you might think. To illustrate this, let me take you on a journey back to 1880 with a Frenchman named Francois Gouin. Here you will see that immersion, without the five principles in mind, still leads to failure. In fact, I have taught thousands of students English within the U.S., and those who fail (and there have been many) consistently fall into two major traps that this story will soon illustrate.

Francois Gouin wanted to learn German, and decided that a year in Germany would be just the thing. At the time of his trip to Germany, you would have found a rather well groomed, young, confident Francois Gouin, who, despite his young age, is already a gifted Latin and Greek professor.

With language learning already part of his career, he is encouraged by his advisors at the College of Caen to follow his pursuit of German by finishing his studies at the University of Berlin. He listens to their advice, and decides that a year spent in nearby Hamburg will give him the time he needs to master German before finishing his studies. Excited with his prospects, Gouin takes his determination and suitcases, and sets off for Hamburg.

FIRST FAILURE

Once in beautiful Hamburg, with its busy thoroughfares, countless shops, and bustling academic centers, Gouin unpacks his suitcases, and immediately begins his language journey.

He spends the first 10 days in seclusion studying in his room. With him, he has a grammar book and a dictionary. He believes languages are learned using "the classical process," a process he says he used for mastering Latin and Greek. To Gouin, the classical process is the study of language through "an acquaintance of its forms." In other words, to learn a language, he feels it best to faithfully study grammar and vocabulary!

After ten days of seclusion, he feels supremely confident, and is anxious to try out his skills. To experiment with his new knowledge, he decides to visit some university classes. Any guesses how that went? Well, Gouin is in for a surprise.

Here are his own words: "But alas! In vain did I strain my ears; in vain my eye strove to interpret the slightest movements of the lips of the professor; in vain I passed from the first classroom to a second; not a word, not a single word would penetrate to my understanding."

SECOND FAILURE

Gouin is understandably upset, but he is determined to get it right. He still feels confident in the 'classical' process, but reasons to himself that there is a missing ingredient in his studies. He decides that he should memorize roots, just as he once did tackling Greek. He reasons that memorizing roots, those basic building blocks of meaning, is the key! He searches for bookstores throughout the streets of Hamburg, and after a long search, comes across a book of German roots put together by a Jesuit priest.

According to Gouin, the book is perfectly organized. Satisfied with the book, back to his room he goes, and he spends four days with it and memorizes somewhere between 800-900 roots. He then spends another four days to review his trusty grammar book and 248 irregular verbs. How does he feel about it all? This time he feels even more certain of victory.

He states, "This time I thought I really possessed the foundation of the language, as well as the laws and the secret of its forms, regular and irregular."

To assure himself of his victory, back to the university he goes, but to his great surprise, once again he understands nothing. As you can imagine, he is freshly upset, and he writes about it in painful terms. He states, "This was no longer a mere deception - it was a failure; nay, it was more than this, it was defeat."

For a moment, Gouin decides perhaps he has gotten it wrong. He wonders if maybe he should try a new technique. He briefly engages in some conversations with his host, a hairdresser, and her patrons. He does this by creating pre-prepared sentences and paying close attention around him so that he can contribute. As a result, they laugh at him, they mock him, and ultimately, they make him feel dumb. He decides not to speak again.

THE PRODIGAL SON

So now what? Gouin returns to his former habits, for months continuing a steady diet of isolated classical lessons. In addition to both his dictionary and grammar book, he now adds to his regiment the translation of large passages of Goethe and Schiller. Slowly and painfully, he chews on his self-prescribed diet of classical methods. In fact, Gouin decides to double down on classical methods and comes up with a final ambitious strategy: memorize an entire dictionary. He reasons:

"Therefore, if I could assimilate the whole dictionary, with the 30,000 words it contains, there was every evidence that, every term being no longer a sound but an idea, I should be able to follow and understand every conversation, read every book, and, by reason of this double exercise, arrive in a very short space of time at being able to speak fluently myself."

Gouin does just as he hopes, and memorizes the dictionary. This may be hard to believe, but let his explanation of the process demonstrate the lengths he was willing to go.

This is what he did. His dictionary was three hundred pages long, so he prescribed himself ten pages a day for thirty days. By the end of the first week, he had learned thousands of words, and by the end of the second week, he memorized 15,000. Finally, after 3-4 weeks of horribly tedious work, he writes about his success. "*Vici!*" he proclaims. Victory! He has done what few of us could imagine doing. He has an entire database of German language, all 30,000 words of a dictionary, in his head. Now, finally, after months of grueling effort, there is nothing more to do but demonstrate his linguistic achievement by going one more time to the university.

Put yourself in his shoes as you walk up the steps of the university. You see the columns on either side of the main entrance. They are majestic. You walk past them. You are smiling to yourself. You have just done something that few people in the world could possibly have done. Now it is time to listen to every single word and relish in your understanding. How could you possibly not understand now? You know, after all, every word! You move purposefully down a hall with a strut in your step, enter a lecture hall, and sit down with near glee. Then your world crashes.

"Not a word! Not a single word!" he says again, as it slowly dawns on him that he has failed for a third time. From lecture hall to lecture hall he inches closer and closer to a hard reality: He has wasted an entire year of his life. For some time, Gouin wonders if perhaps he cannot learn languages. However, a stronger thought starts to overtake him. He starts to feel, well, betrayed. Could his teachers--the very masters he trusted---have been wrong? Could he be learning language incorrectly?

Gouin begins to suspect something he would not have suspected earlier: that those who walk the marbled halls of academia might not actually know what they are talking about! It was a heretical thought, but, given his circumstances, it was the only thought that remained. His method of learning, his strategies, simply do not work.

Without the five questions in mind, even immersion fails.

9

THE TWO TRAPS

I TOOK FIVE YEARS OF SPANISH IN JUNIOR HIGH AND high school, and got A's in all my classes. Like Gouin, I rarely if ever practiced outside the classroom at all, and so I had very little ability to communicate. I was clueless in my approach to language learning.

Let me explain just how clueless. Would you believe that I have a mother who is from Mexico and speaks perfect Spanish? Why did I never think of asking her to help me with my homework? How about my father? My father, although not a native Spanish speaker, was the second-best thing. He is an excellent Spanish speaker and at one time taught Spanish at the junior high and high school level. On top of that, I had a dozen friends, including my high school crush, who spoke Spanish fluently. Why in the world would I choose to study in isolation instead of just jumping in the pool?

Two phenomena, or traps, help explain my behavior. The first I will refer to as the classroom trap. The classroom trap is the faulty belief that the classroom is a world unto itself, and the strategies used inside it either do not apply to the real world, or do not *yet* apply to the real world. In some sense, there is a belief that the one exists separate from the other. Think of Gouin again. He believed that knowledge was first obtained alone in a room even though he was in Germany, and only after leaving his room did he attempt to test his knowledge. *In other words, he thought his room was a laboratory, rather than using the world around him as a laboratory.*

Now let us discuss the second trap. Stephen Krashen, a famous language-learning expert, hypothesizes that language learners have negative emotions when they are learning a language, and that these emotions impede their ability to receive the necessary input. He calls this an "affective filter," meaning that your emotions filter, or prevent, information from coming in. When your emotions are high, the filter is high and you learn less. When you are relaxed and feel confident, the filter is low and you learn more information.

Now let us think back to Gouin. By his own account, at the university and in the hairdresser shop, Gouin experienced feelings of discomfort when trying to listen to or speak with Germans. He did not want to be embarrassed or look foolish. In fact, I believe this may be *precisely* because he was such a smart, successful academic. This is the second trap, one we will refer to as the Gouin effect.

The Gouin effect stems from the desire to maintain one's appearance or social standing. We may feel this effect especially when we are around those who speak a language better than we do. Interestingly, the Gouin effect, these feelings of discomfort because we are not used to looking stupid, can and often lead us right back to the classroom trap.

Consider my own story. Why did I never speak to my mother, my father, or my crush? As a straight A student who prided myself on my academic abilities, it was hard for me to want to look foolish, and especially in front of my parents or my teenage crush.

So, do I recommend immersion? Absolutely. However, when we talk of immersion, I need it to be clear that immersion without the five questions will also lead to failure. Furthermore, and perhaps most importantly, if you keep the five questions in mind, you will discover the most amazing thing: immersion can happen just about anywhere. No matter where you are in the world, immersion can and is happening in your own backyard.

Overcoming your fear of looking stupid is a key to your success.

THE ECOSYSTEM: WHY?

Developing a language ecosystem is the single most important key to a modern approach to language learning. I have seen thousands of people do it, although many of them are unaware of what they are doing. This is because developing an ecosystem is often something that comes naturally; something that comes out of sheer curiosity about the world. Successful learners generally search out and fall in love with music, movies, books, and people from different cultures, and thus, never realize that the nature of their love is what has given them the desire to keep going.

While I will explain later how to create a language ecosystem, let me begin with the more fundamental question. Why is this approach so much more successful?

One answer has to do with motivation. Developing a language ecosystem rarely feels like work. This is because making real connections is exciting. In fact, it tends to give someone an attitude of being an explorer, searching out and finding hidden treasures throughout the world. This attitude of exploration and discovery is naturally more motivating. By letting curiosity and creativity drive you, you will stumble upon something I call "happy accidents."

A happy accident occurs when you find a language resource that is interesting—even wonderful—and well suited to your level and interests. For me, for example, I discovered that I could learn beginning French by watching native French speakers read Eric Carle books translated into French. I love Eric Carle books, and at the time, the simplicity was perfect for my level. I also found a series of short films by a French filmmaker. These brief videos were fun for me to watch multiple times, and I could watch subtitles to help me understand.

I also started to search for French-speaking companions. I went online and simply asked if anyone knew French, and I was surprised to discover that several of my own friends spoke French. I began to send basic messages in my broken French, and they were gracious enough to respond and give me pointers.

I even found a new friend online, a French speaker from Haiti, who has proven to be a great resource because of his willingness to ask me questions (forcing me to elaborate), correct my errors, and push me out of my comfort zone. He even sent me a link to a cool documentary on Haiti, which I shared with my family. For the first time ever, my family members showed interest in traveling there.

Since my French was so poor, finding books was a bit trickier for me, but as I went exploring, I discovered I had a copy of *The Little Prince* in English. I reasoned that maybe, just maybe, I could read the French version alongside it.

I located a French copy in an online store, and soon, I was reading in French. It was tough, and I often went back to the English, took notes, and to my delight, understood enough that it was fun to re-read. In fact, I shared some of my thoughts online, and even started something of a reader's circle.

I also began watching French movies on Netflix, and fell upon a series of movies from a particular actress, Audrey Tatou, whom I adore. I even invited my wife and daughter to watch one of her movies. My 12-year old daughter complained about the subtitles at the beginning, but soon got lost in the story and loved the movie.

Developing this basic language ecosystem is liberating. By stepping away from a single book or commercial product, I realized I was on top of a huge, bloated commercial market, rather than stuck beneath it. From this I learned a basic truth. As long as you know basic language learning principles, the kind we will discuss in this book, the person best suited at choosing a curriculum…is you.

Real connections do not feel like work.

THE ECOSYSTEM: WHAT?

WHILE AN ECOSYSTEM IS A SIMPLE CONCEPT, THERE ARE A FEW things to keep in mind. To begin, good language learners surround themselves with language in such a natural way that it does not feel like a system as much as a way of life. Of course we binge-watch *Anne of Green Gables* in Spanish, I tell my children. "That's just how it is." After a while, they do not even question it. In fact, my children once watched an episode in English and proclaimed the Spanish version much better. "We just like the voices," they said. *Perfect*, I thought.

To construct a language ecosystem, you will need some basic principles that can transform your home into a language friendly arena, a place where another culture is simply a given part of who you are. Here are five quick tips to get you started. At the end of this book, you will find worksheets to help you try each one.

TIP 1: GO ON LANGUAGE MISSIONS (GATHER AND UTILIZE RESOURCES)

The concept of exploring is at the center of this chapter for good reason. Your mission (should you choose to accept it) is to find and gather resources that are potential candidates for your language ecosystem. It is not unlike going shopping for furniture, in that you want to find items that will match your personal preference and lifestyle in a natural way. As you search for items to "add" to your ecosystem, you will want to consider how well they function in your life or home.

I have noticed that a number of resources are good for a short time, but that I grow tired of them quickly. Other resources, on the other hand, have become almost daily routines for me. They are simply ways in which I engage with the world.

For example, one temporary resource for me was Duolingo, an online app that gave me two thousand words in French. I found that it was difficult to get through, but I liked the gamified aspects of it. After a while, however, I realized that it was not getting me to communicate or function well in French.

On the other hand, I found a podcast called *Le Journal en Français Facile* (the news in easy French) that I like to hear every day on my way to work. I like to find out what is happening in the world, and while I miss quite a bit of information with some topics, there are transcripts online that allow me to review the vocabulary I did not understand. It is perfect for both my level and my lifestyle. I plan to keep this resource with me for quite some time.

You might be wondering how one begins a search to find resources. I primarily use search engines, social media, streaming video, and music to look for resources that might work. I am not the only one, however, who has learned to keep an eye out for resources.

Since inviting many of my own friends to learn a language

with me, many people now send me links to things I might like. By letting people know that I am on a language mission, often there is a contagious effect. I find that when I show my own enthusiasm toward learning a language, people love to be generous.

TIP 2: JOIN A LANGUAGE-LEARNING NETWORK

Speaking of people, one of the most essential strategies in forming a language ecosystem is finding the right people to join you on your journey. I call this "forming a language learning network." I mentioned that there are people who love to help me find resources, and these individuals are definitely members of my network. However, they are not the only members. In fact, many people play distinct roles in the language ecosystem concept. First, whenever possible, I like to find family and friends to serve as real time, face-to-face speaking companions.

When I cannot find a face-to-face companion, I search online, looking for anyone that might be interested in the language. I often find two kinds of helpful companions. Fluent speakers are excellent sources of feedback (they can correct my errors), and they often are willing to do so in exchange for practicing one of the languages I speak.

While fluent speakers are an excellent resource, I also find that fellow language learners, people who are learning the language just like me, are more patient conversation partners. Finally, I often find that people who share my same interests (say, French cooking, for example), can be excellent companions for listening and speaking practice.

TIPS 3, 4, AND 5: PREDICT, PREPARE, AND PERFORM

One way learners misunderstand the language ecosystem concept is that they think their only job is to collect resources.

While collecting resources is important, the resources are of little use unless utilized. I have observed that many individuals gather resources as a sort of crutch, and my best guess is that they suffer from the Gouin effect to some degree. Instead of practicing the knowledge they are acquiring, they tell themselves that they just need to gather more resources until they feel comfortable. Gouin himself, you will remember, believed that collecting and memorizing vocabulary would allow him to burst into conversation spontaneously, so he never learned to command the vocabulary he was collecting.

Let me suggest three strategies to help you turn your resources into practice tasks. This series of strategies I refer to as **predict**, **prepare**, and **perform**.

Imagine that you want to have a conversation about a show you just watched. The first step in having a useful conversation (either online or in person) is to think ahead of time what will likely be said. You will want to think about the words from the show and words that might help the conversation along. You will want to think about questions people might ask you, and you will want to ask questions of your own. In other words, one of the most important parts of creating dialogue is to think about it ahead of time. This skill, imagining what to say in a future conversation, we will refer to as *predicting*.

The next technique is called *preparation*. Imagine that you have now predicted what you might say about the show in a conversation, and even went through the bother of writing down answers to five or six questions. However, that does not mean that you can suddenly speak quickly or fluidly just because you wrote things down. To become more confident in your ability, you need to turn your prediction into preparation. This is done by practicing before the actual event, often multiple times in front of a mirror, the shower, the car, or anywhere else. I like to fill out conversation cards on certain topics, review those cards several times, and find a quiet place to internalize the conversation. For me, proper preparation gives me the courage and ability to overcome my fear and can even make me excited to try.

After you feel sufficiently prepared, it is time to *perform*. After you have prepared for a conversation, you will want to test out your preparation with a partner. If you are still feeling a bit shy, you might want to try a non-native speaker of the language. You will notice that every performance is imperfect, and sometimes you might stumble quite a bit. That's okay. In fact, approach these moments as "field testing," meaning that these are meant to give you an idea of where you stand. In fact, I often take notes after a performance on what I did well and what I need to improve. By thinking of performance in this fashion, I come away with an improved outlook.

These three strategies, predict, prepare, and perform, are important final steps to the explorer approach. They will give you a clear path to utilizing the resources you are gathering.

As an explorer, you must seek for treasure in the form of movies, music, websites, and people.

∾

To overcome the Gouin effect, you must practice with the materials you find as quickly as possible.

THE ECOSYSTEM: HOW?

IMAGINE THAT A BUSINESS WANTS TO CREATE A LANGUAGE ecosystem for their employees. For example, let us say that a Japanese-owned company in the United States wants their upper-middle management to speak Japanese. Management has seen that better knowledge of Japanese allows for greater workflow, and each month, many essential trainings and documents from the Tokyo office are given only in Japanese. Earlier, management had tried to give employees free Japanese classes, but motivation for these classes declined rapidly. Upon learning about the language ecosystem concept, they wonder if something more natural and integrated could occur. They decide to create a language ecosystem in the workplace to encourage the speaking of Japanese.

They first, wisely, identify what resources they have. They have

1. the Japanese materials sent from headquarters each month,

2. a pair of Japanese native speakers who work in upper management, and

3. several Americans who have learned Japanese to an intermediate level.

This group discusses ideas on how to make the workplace more Japanese friendly and come up with a series of tasks and resources. They decide on a conversation hour each day during breaks where they can help others understand and break down the most vital company trainings. As lovers of all things Japanese, they dedicate a room to Japanese music, food, and culture, and invite employees to spend time in that room during breaks. In addition, they create a website with several activities and resources that employees can look at for their own personal study. Furthermore, they find an online language course, Japanese Pod 101, and think about making an investment in it.

This example is typical to designs I have seen put in place in many companies. I admit that I find it an improvement over the previous model of just giving "Japanese classes"; however, this model can be greatly improved if the company would consider a system of incentives. In other words, the company understands why they should do a language ecosystem, and understand what an ecosystem is, but they still lack a proper understanding of *how* it should be done.

Incentives are the driving force behind a language ecosystem's momentum, and the correct incentive is everything. I tend to find that the best incentives are, once again, the most natural ones.

For instance, in our company example, if management believes strongly that Japanese ability increases productivity, the company might offer a bonus if employees improve their Japanese significantly within a given year. In addition, employees who want promotions in the company should know that Japanese is a highly desirable skill, and this information should be clear (at the very least, available on job descriptions).

Other ideas might include reimbursements for those who successfully complete the online course, or even small incentives, like free lunches for those who participate in the conversation hour.

In other words, language learning increases when people are taught that their efforts have value. In fact, imagine how incentivizing it might be if the boss, finally catching on to the idea of incentives, offered two round trip tickets to Japan for the employee who showed the greatest improvement!

While the analogy is not perfect, let us apply this idea to your personal language-learning ecosystem. First, you are both the CEO and employee. As CEO, you will have to be wise about the investments you are willing to make, whereas, as an employee, you will have to consider which investments would actually motivate you.

So, what motivates you? When discussing a rewards-based incentive, think of ways in which you would like to pay yourself for both short-term and long-term commitments.

Give yourself a small reward for a small commitment kept, and a larger reward for larger commitments. A small reward, like completing a single lesson plan, might be to check social media, eat a donut, or walk the dog. A long-term commitment, like completing a course, might receive a larger reward, like tickets to a movie. Perhaps you want to move from a beginning to intermediate level of a certain language. Why not offer yourself tickets to your dream vacation as soon as you pass the test? Now that is motivating!

Motivate your language learning progress with a series of incentives.

12.5 NOT EVEN A CHAPTER, JUST A FREE OFFER

My colleague Justin Shewell and I have created a book called *50 Ways to Learn a Language*. In it, we identify small, research-tested methods to build a language ecosystem. In our companion website, we offer a free resource called "The Randomizer," which will give you one of these fifty strategies each day to help guide your study. If you are a little stuck, and simply do not know what to do on any given day, try the randomizer:

http://www.language-warriors.com/randomizer

QUESTIONS FOR GROUP DISCUSSION

1. Have you ever felt like Francois Gouin? What is it about his experience that feels familiar to you?
2. Have you ever gone on a language mission? What was it like and how did it feel? How did you choose your task?

3. Do you use the "predict/prepare/perform" method in any other aspect of your life? How has it proven useful?

4. What motivates you to get things done? What motivates you to learn a language?

PART III
INTROSPECT

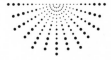

To see a world in a grain of sand and heaven in a wild flower / Hold infinity in the palm of your hand and eternity in an hour.

— WILLIAM BLAKE

13

INNERSPACE

THE ECOSYSTEM IS LIKE A POOL. IMAGINE THAT THE resources you discover are like water that can fill a pool, and before too long, you fill the pool enough so that you can swim. While the chance to swim in this newly created pool excites you, what might happen if you fill that pool without ever taking any swim lessons? How might you feel about the pool then? Even if you build an excellent pool, if you do not know how to swim, you will find yourself gasping for breath and wanting out. While the ecosystem concept is a powerful one, it does not work very well unless, metaphorically, you know how to swim.

I would like you to meet a bright-eyed Kurdish student of mine with an unconquerable spirit. One day, however, she could not take the pressure that comes with learning a language and found herself drowning in the pool she herself had created. Her story taught me that exploring the outside world is not enough.

In language learning, you must constantly look inward.

~

PIECES, BY NIGAR AZIZ

When I came to the U.S., I was so, so sad at the beginning. You know, in my country, we have ridiculous comedies—comedies that meant nothing to me when I was in Kurdistan. Now in the U.S., I watch them and fall off my chair laughing. I have forgotten how funny my people are. I have forgotten many things.

Forgetting things. Now that I am in the United States, I am constantly forgetting things, like the glass table I had at my old home. While it was beautiful, it became part of my everyday life, and after a while, I forgot it was special to me. One day, carelessly, I tossed my keys on the table and it broke into pieces.

Now, I often think about how my home is that glass table. Since arriving in the U.S, I remember different pieces of my home life, and each piece I find is like a discovery. I remember my cousins laughing, a tree in my front yard, or my mother's embrace as I return from school. Each piece has such value to me now! I spend hours gathering the broken pieces of my past.

For these last few years, I have attempted to do whatever is best for my country. I know the Kurdish people need someone to stand up for them, so that is why I have decided to become a top lawyer and educator, all of which led me to come to the United States. I knew that a U.S. degree was the key for my dream to become real. It was not fun, easy, or simple, but along with my husband, I decided, and we left our homeland to accomplish our dreams.

Yet one night, in the bitterness of this self-imposed exile in the United States, I told my husband, "I want to stop." He stared at me as if I was joking. This was, after all, our dream. I explained, "I want to stop. Stop because I cannot tolerate and endure this situation." That night, I cried and would not stop crying until I looked in front of the mirror. I saw my eyes. I saw how red they were, but more than that, I saw a child, a crying, stubborn child.

Like a crazy person, I talked with myself, and this was not the first time. Sometimes it was in front of the mirror, as if I were speaking to someone from my imagination. Not a real person, but someone that wanted me to see beyond the obstacles I was seeing.

"What do you want, Nigar?"

"I want to go home."

"Why? Do you want to be lazy? They need you. They need you. I thought you wanted to sacrifice big things. I thought you wanted to sacrifice it all. There are bigger things than you." The girl on the other side of the mirror stared at me with suspicious eyes.

"But I'm so tired."

"Nigar, what are you doing? You look like a crazy person, staring at me crying like that. Have you no strength? Why did you choose this?"

"But I didn't know…"

"You DID know. You did know it would be hard. Did you choose the United States just for fun? For travel? Think about that. Just think."

I stare at myself in the mirror. The girl's hands are in fists. I want to tell her that I just wanted to go home. I want her to understand, but her eyes show me she is in no mood to give sympathy. What did she ask me to do? Oh, that is right. She wants me to think, so I begin to think. I look at the girl in the mirror again and she seems so different from me: confident, angry, able to do anything, and accepting only my best. In my mind, I realize that I have given her a name, and that the name is American. I cannot quite explain how I know, but I know her name is Tina. I decide to avoid her and speak to myself.

"Okay, Nigar," I whisper to myself, "What do you want right now?" I know immediately that my answer is to return to my country. I do not look at Tina, and I only whisper to myself, but Tina has overheard me.

"So that's it, then? You want to return to your country, have fun, and relax? No more studies, huh? So, you want to go back and start having some fun?No more studying? No more working hard? You want this?"

I respond to her, "Yes. Life is, well, it is so short. I don't want to...have any...any responsibilities. This life is too hard. I can't do it. I can't do it, Tina."

"Oh," she taunts me with a false sympathetic smile, "I thought you were a strong person and that you wanted to *sacrifice* yourself for your country. You said you would do it. You were so confident then. Well, now, unfortunately, we find out the truth: you are a selfish person. You are a really selfish person."

I scream at her, "No, no, I am not! But I..."I cannot finish my thought. Tina already has an answer.

"It's okay. I understand. You want to relax and let other people suffer from corruption. It is not your fault you were born into a rich country with disadvantaged people and a bad government. Why should you be needy? Why should you suffer? I understand."

I want to scream at Tina. I look into the mirror and want to break the glass. I am tired of her self-righteous strength. Then she does something different. She changes her approach and begins speaking of the job I left behind as a law teacher. She reminds me of the very reason I left the country.

"How about your future students? How about them?"

I try to answer, "If I die after 5 years, I did nothing in my life, just difficulties and depression, and that's the end of me. I am so sad. I cannot tolerate this situation. Why do you say I am selfish? I am not selfish."

I want to tell Tina that I do not even know academic terms in English, terms I know I will need in my classes. I have tried memorizing lists. I have tried reading articles. I have written down essay topics and given speeches aloud in my living room. I want to tell her that nothing works. Especially those dumb lists. They have never worked for me.

Tina knows better. She knows that I have made progress. She has been watching carefully and knows which strategies have worked, and which have not. She is constantly looking for advantages, constantly adding new resources and strategies. She even tells me how she knows that the lists are not working, but that the conversation groups are. She knows that I have more ability because of my willingness to talk with students over homework assignments and taking those lists to the conversation groups has worked to get me to practice memorized words. She sees another opportunity to mix strategies, to adjust, to become better. Part of me still does not want to become better. I just want to go home.

Now I am thinking about home in a different way. Tina has a way of doing this to me. Now I reflect on those students. The future of our country. Those students had hope, even in a system that was filled with decades of corruption. They believed that we could change the country. I had left the country with my husband knowing that if we learned how the legal system should work, then we could return and fight.

Tina keeps speaking and I am listening now. "How about your future students? How about them? They need a teacher, a friend. They need you. How about them? Can you imagine the looks on their faces and in their eyes?"

I do remember the looks on the faces of students in Kurdistan. I do remember their eyes. I cannot imagine forgetting them, but I suddenly realize I have. I concentrate and try to remember some of their names. I think of their faces—like the lovely girl who wore a headscarf and was always reading. She always came after class and asked my advice. What was her name? Once again, I realize that I have become careless. I stand for a long time trying to remember. I begin to see more faces, more names, until finally I am satisfied. I do not know how long it takes, but I feel whole again and I open my eyes. I had not even realized they were closed, but when I open them, I see Tina looking at me.

"You are right, Tina. I remember now." She stares at me with a small grin. After a while, it turns into a big smile. I feel my heart spill out like water. I am thankful for my imaginary friend.

"I won't break any more glass today," I tell her.

Then, without words, I promise myself, and Tina, that I will not be careless anymore when I see something so beautiful as a glass table. As I look in the mirror again, I see that Tina and I are now somehow the same person. Confident. Able to do anything. Accepting only my best.

I do not know when it happened, but she has become a part of me.

14

THE LONG AND SHORT OF
MOTIVATION

Isn't Nigar amazing? Her story has moved and motivated people throughout the world, and her sheer grit and willingness to overcome is something I saw everyday as a student in my class.

Nigar's story, however, is perhaps more remarkable than a typical language learner. Truthfully, most learners do not have to give up friends and family on a quest to learn a language. While her circumstances may be unique, the patterns she must go through are instructive for all learners. My experience has led me to believe that language learners all tend to go through spells of intense motivation, and eventually experience a loss of that motivation.

Let us discuss where Nigar's story can be instructive and illustrate common patterns that you can use.

First, like many of us, Nigar loses her nerve. She starts to focus on the difficulties of learning a language, and the loss of family and friends that she feels. Yet despite the sacrifice she is feeling, she tries to re-center herself by reflecting on her primary motivation. While looking at herself in the mirror, she is trying to find her truest self. Her core reason for doing what she is doing.

Nigar, confronted with her alter ego Tina, realizes that her main goal is centered on her students. She wants to help them, and even realizes she has forgotten their names. For Nigar, this is an important moment because it is an act of motivation, and her strategy, that of trying to remember her core goals and values is instructive.

Researchers agree. Studies have demonstrated that some of the best language learners keep their goals at the forefront, and are simply better at knowing, and remembering, what their long-term goals are (Brown, 2002; Dörnyei, Z. & Csizer, K., 1998). In other words, if you find yourself ever losing your nerve, it may be an important time for you to re-center yourself and remember the primary reason you are learning a language.

As you consider your own primary or long-term goal, remember that this kind of goal is a fundamental driving reason for learning a language. It is often imaginary, such as *I can see myself talking with my grandmother back in Germany* or intriguing, like *I want to backpack through Switzerland* or *I want to spend a summer in Spain*, and it might even be called romantic in the classical sense, such as *I want to present my findings on Chinese burial rituals at a conference in China*. Although imaginary, it generally has a specific timeline: *Before my daughter graduates, I want to take her to Japan*. Above all, your goal is something that drives you forward, and keeps you on task when other language learners generally stop.

Sometimes, however, your long-term goals may feel too out of reach. It is at times like these that you may want to reflect on short-term goals and successes. In other words, while you may think to yourself, "I'm never going to be able to master 500 kanji this summer," you might say to yourself instead, "I will learn three kanji today." In that light, in the next chapter, we'll discuss the idea of going on short, motivational "language missions."

When you experience a loss of motivation, let long-term goals motivate you. When long-term motivation doesn't work, focus on a short-term success.

GOING ON LANGUAGE MISSIONS

NIGAR'S STORY IS NOT JUST INSTRUCTIVE BECAUSE OF HER ability to motivate herself; she also teaches us the importance of evaluating and adjusting the tasks and strategies she is using. Notice what she says here:

Tina knows...I have made progress. She has been watching carefully and knows which strategies have worked, and which have not. She is constantly looking for advantages, constantly adding new resources and strategies. She even tells me how she knows that the lists are not working, but that the conversation groups are. She knows that I have more ability because of my willingness to talk with students over homework assignments, and taking those lists to the conversation groups has worked to get me to practice memorized words. She sees another opportunity to mix strategies, to adjust, to become better.

This kind of evaluation and adjustment is the second kind of self-reflection, one that prompts you to consider if your strategies are helping you learn. Nigar has noticed that the studying of lists isn't really paying off, but that when the technique of memorizing words is added to conversation groups, she is learning. In other words, Nigar has given herself a language task and completes it, but doesn't stop there. She reviews, reflects, and adjusts her task, and as a result, improves her outcome.

Before we discuss how to adjust language tasks, let's discuss what a language task is. A series of studies in the 1970s and 80s discovered that the best learners love to give themselves tasks. Now referred to as the "good language learner" studies, these series of observations and experimental evidence attempted to discover what good language learners do that make them, well, good language learners. Near or at the top of most researchers' list was the fact that good language learners had an "active task approach."

For these researchers, the idea of an active task approach meant many different things, but typically it centered around the idea that language learners are willing to try out new things, almost as if they were assigning themselves a lot of different kinds of homework.

Sometimes I like to refer to tasks or homework as *challenges* or *language missions*. This is because I want learners to constantly remember that language study is an adventure outside the confines of your own private study.

Many researchers, however, have settled on the term *task* or *language task*, which Michael Long defines accordingly:

> [a language task is] a piece of work undertaken for oneself or for others, freely or for some reward. Thus, examples of tasks include [. . .] filling out a form, buying a pair of shoes, making an airline reservation, borrowing a library book, taking a driving test, typing a letter, [. . .], making a hotel reservation, writing a check, finding a street destination and helping someone across the road. (p. 89)

In other words, language tasks refer to things we do in everyday life, at work, at play, and in between. Notice how these tasks don't feel like things that happen within a classroom, but rather connect you to the world outside.

While some of Long's examples might more easily be accomplished in the host country, you will find that there are thousands of activities you can do to learn a language. As soon as you get the spirit of language missions, you'll find that it can be quite addictive.

HOW TO CHOOSE LANGUAGE MISSIONS

Going on language missions is at the center of the language ecosystem concept. This is because each mission may or may not represent another piece to the ecosystem puzzle you are creating. As you add new tasks, new strategies, new goals, and new resources, you begin to amass a wealth of knowledge about what works—and doesn't work—for you. You'll find not only that you discover fascinating resources such as movies, books, and websites, but you'll also begin to identify strategies as well (scaffold a movie using subtitles and journaling, read a book using side-by-side or parallel text).

This, however, can be tricky at first. You may not know what strategies are available to you, and you may choose ones that have been proven unproductive and simply not know it.

Here are three tips to get you started:

1. **Know the difference between tasks and strategies.** As you reflect on the tasks that you give yourself, you might be quick to assume that if something didn't work for you once, it is not worth considering again. Here we want you to recognize that often tasks may not work at first, but may work sometime later. Furthermore, sometimes the task is good, but the strategy is not. Let's define the terms

task and strategy to help explain. A task refers to an activity, like watching a movie, while a strategy refers to something that helps you know how to perform the task, like watching a movie *with subtitles in your language.* The difference may be subtle, but it can have huge implications. For example, as you evaluate this activity, you may wrongly believe that watching a movie is a bad idea because you watched one with subtitles and came away with nothing. Language learners know that watching with subtitles often doesn't work for beginners because they tend to tune out the target language. However, there are techniques that can be paired with movie watching that are perfect for beginning learners. In other words, *the task was fine, but the strategy needed to be adjusted.* Please be aware that there are strategies for beginning, intermediate, and advanced learners, and that a variety of tools (strategies) can help you select how to make the task be the most beneficial for you.

2. **Get acquainted with your options.** I recommend going on language missions right away, and I recommend the randomizer on http://www.language-warriors.com to get you started. There you will find over 50 examples of both tasks and strategies that are an essential part of a new ecosystem. Another way to get involved in language missions, however, is through the Language Map. The Language Map is my absolute favorite way for learners to develop an ecosystem and connect to a worldwide community. I'll talk about that resource at the end of part III. Oh, and don't forget! There are many workbook pages in the back of the book to help you engage in strategies that match the different sections of the book.

3. **Lead with fun!** I cannot emphasize enough how language learning must always be attached to having a great time. The more you find resources, tasks, and strategies that are exciting, the more you will stick with your studies and create an ecosystem that is truly vibrant. I have noticed that when someone truly gets the ecosystem concept, a light turns on. It is a truly addicting way to learn a language, and to be honest, I can't imagine not having language learning ecosystems be a part of who I am for the rest of my life. When you have an ecosystem that truly works, you are excited to watch the next episode of a show, read a book, discover a new recipe, and engage with fellow learners (not to mention native speakers). You will suddenly see yourself not only wanting to visit one country, but a dozen.

Here are a few thoughts about the language ecosystem concept that might help you realize what it can become in your life:

- A language ecosystem means immersing yourself in a target language in the most engaging, natural way you can.
- A language ecosystem allows you to discover people and events, often people you already know and events happening just around the corner.
- A language ecosystem is a flexible plan of attack; one that bends to your needs and desires.
- A language ecosystem is an invitation to yourself and others to take a series of journeys.
- A language ecosystem unlocks the world around you and connects you to it.

- A language ecosystem is how thousands of people are learning a language.
- A language ecosystem is a way of turbocharging your efforts, incentivizing your successes, and looking forward to what might happen next.

Once you understand what a language ecosystem is, you will never want to stop going on language missions.

16

STRATEGIES FOR BETTER INTROSPECTION

PEOPLE CONSTANTLY THINK ABOUT WHAT THEY ARE DOING right (or wrong) in aspects of their lives: parenting, schooling, the workplace…lawn care.

Okay, let's talk about lawn care; specifically, my lawn, and my inability to care for it. I hate my lawn. It grows wildly in areas I don't want, and there are dead patches throughout it in places that, well, grass should grow. I talk to it. In fact, I admit I have berated it and then begged it for forgiveness in case it was listening. My lawn is obviously making me crazy. There is a section of it that is bone-dry, and two feet to the right there is a section that I call the swamp. The orange tree hates me, too, and as evidence of that, I have a three-inch scar from a thorn when I tried to trim it back. Orange tree does not want to be trimmed.

Yet my relationship with my lawn has not always been like this. It used to be lush. It was a source of pride. My father visited once a few years back and complimented me on it.

"How do you do it?" he asked. (Imagine us on the back porch swigging root beer and appearing manly.)

"I just paid attention to it; figured it out." I said this in a rather smarmy, condescending way, and I imagine that if I were a character in a movie, people would naturally assume I was the know-it-all that has it coming to him. You know, the guy that gets eaten by the dinosaur. Or in this case, the guy that loses to his lawn.

And did I ever. The thing is, though, I know precisely why the lawn has become an eyesore (and possibly the location of a *Honey, I Shrunk the Kids* sequel). It isn't my lawn's fault at all. My failure comes directly from me.

In those golden days of yore when I had it all figured out, there had been a shift in my perspective. Instead of thinking that the lawn was an unpredictable and random mess of problems, I had begun to reason through each task individually. For example, my programmable sprinkler system was overwatering a certain area, and so I reduced the amount of time that the swampy area got watered.

In another section of the lawn, the trampoline blocked out the sun, killing the Bermuda grass and keeping the winter grass alive too long. By moving the trampoline every few days, I made sure the Bermuda was safe from harm.

In short, the more I thought about each problem, the more I realized that the lawn wasn't an impossible set of riddles, it was a predictable ecosystem that simply needed me to think about it.

In fact, the first rule to my success was to stop pretending I couldn't figure it out. I had developed a habit wherein if my wife mentioned a problem about the lawn, I immediately took a defensive position that the lawn was a mysterious and unsolvable riddle, and that I possessed none of the answers. It was as if she had asked me to solve the mysteries of the cosmos or figure out a way to stop our teenager from rolling her eyes.

In life, I imagine we all have a list of things that demand our attention. Whether we like it or not, the attention we pay to each item on the list is often what results in success. The reason I tell this story is because when failure comes knocking at our doorstep, not everyone wants to think about the part they play in the failures they see around them. It is simply easier for me to say that my awful lawn is obviously not my fault. It is just a stupid, angry, spiteful lawn, and it has likely grown self-aware (dear lawn, if this is true, I apologize).

In a similar way, it is crucial that, as you build a language ecosystem, you think of *yourself* as the one responsible for thinking through each problem, each task and strategy. Often, you'll discover that through careful introspection, you'll find an answer. Don't fall into the trap of thinking that nothing can be done, and that you cannot solve the riddle in front of you. It simply isn't true.

Following this line of thinking, here are four strategies that will help you learn how to become more introspective (mostly with language, but possibly with lawns).

JOURNALING

The first strategy is journaling. Journaling is an effective way of taking note of your experiences, both failures and successes. Journaling in this fashion is often called reflective journaling, meaning that your role is that of the scientist or observer. Your job is to take field notes, reflect on what was successful about your tasks (which in this case might best be called experiments) and record them diligently so that you inform your own future tasks, and perhaps others that might follow your own path.

Francois Gouin's biography, for example, helps us understand the unsuccessful strategies he used while in Hamburg. His later successes are also recorded and are a valuable addition to language acquisition researchers and learners everywhere.

MONITORING

The strategy of monitoring is a broad strategy that can be used in association with many other tasks and strategies. Monitoring, in its simplest form, simply means observing your own speech or writing, but may be specifically applied to a unique grammatical structure, a list of vocabulary, a discrete sound, or any other linguistic item. In other words, many people wisely choose to monitor only one aspect of their language performance rather than every possible element.

The purpose of monitoring is to evaluate your current ability to perform the language element that you choose to monitor. For example, if you have decided to work on a certain sound that is difficult for you (say the trilled "r" in Spanish), you would pay close attention to that sound as you speak.

Some choose to monitor by recording themselves, giving them a chance to observe more closely the elements that they do well or poorly. While it may be uncomfortable to record yourself, it can give you vital insights as to what you are doing right and wrong.

SUMMARIZING

A very simple but often underutilized strategy is summarizing. Summarizing is a powerful technique that can be used to retain information. A great many studies suggest that after studying, recalling what you have just learned by either speaking to a partner or writing down what you have studied helps the brain make needed synaptic connections. If you don't have a partner or pad and paper available, one powerful way to summarize is through a think aloud.

THINK ALOUD

As the name suggests, this strategy invites learners to think out loud and reflect on their own learning. In other words, a think aloud is often used to think about how things are going. When used this way, a think aloud is a metacognitive strategy, meaning that you are thinking about your thinking, or at least reflecting on your own learning. I often begin this kind of think aloud by saying, "So I am trying to learn Arabic by…" I then state what I like or don't like about the task and/or strategy I have chosen. I then summarize how things are going.

You can also use think alouds to monitor your own speech production. This kind of think aloud invites you to have imaginary conversations with yourself. Crazy? Perhaps. Yet by having these imaginary conversations learners can see if they have the sufficient vocabulary and grammar to speak on a topic.

A classic example would be pretending you are at a French restaurant and ordering a meal in French. By imagining the questions asked and answered, you are performing a think aloud that will help you monitor your own progress and discover areas where you might need to improve. You may not want to do a think aloud in public, perhaps, but I find that the shower and my car are two of my favorite places to monitor my own speech with a think aloud. If my wife catches me talking in the shower, I can always blame it on the lawn.

～

One last note about my lawn. I have noticed that, as with all things, we often shift priorities as demands on our attention change. And we justify our failures this way. No doubt I am very tempted to tell myself that I am a very busy fellow, too busy to worry about that broken sprinkler head that is spilling gallons upon gallons of water down my driveway each day. *Sorry, lawn. You just don't make the cut,* I tell myself.

While there is truth to the idea that we have limited amounts of time, what I have also learned is that ecosystems, when they are running well, often take less time and management when we give them even a little concern compared to the time we spend on what happens when we let them fall into a state of disrepair. In other words, the great thing about ecosystems is that, if you set them up right, they do most of the work on their own.

> *If you put in the work and develop your ecosystem properly, language learning occurs naturally, without effort.*

16.5 NOT EVEN A CHAPTER, JUST SOMETHING COOL

I have always wanted to be Indiana Jones. He is just so cool with that hat, whip, and gun. Watching the Indiana Jones movies when I was young made me feel like the world was filled with opportunities, and that treasure might be found in any corner of the world.

Sadly, I'm not Indiana Jones, and my adventure-seeking days are limited by bad knees and a mortgage. Before you feel sorry for me, however, the truth is that I love my Arizona desert lifestyle with my wife and four kids. I enjoy coming home in the afternoons, spending time with my family, and going, well, nowhere.

Yet lately adventure seems to be finding me. You see, with the creation of my own language ecosystems, I have become connected to people all over the world, and I communicate weekly with people from the most fascinating places (this last week it was Azerbaijan, Senegal, and Haiti). Without having to travel or even work too hard, I have made friends all over the world by going on mini-language missions.

Can you imagine yourself taking mini-language missions and

connecting with people? I hope you can. Whether you are the kind of person that has never known how to learn a language, or someone who is eager to join a group of like-minded language lovers, I strongly urge you to try The Language Map.

The Language Map is an ecosystem-building tool that will take you on 12 different adventures with four mini-language missions in each adventure. Each mini-language mission will teach you strategies and tasks to add to your language ecosystem. The map also has video instructions implanted in a QR code to describe each mission (cleverly placed within each illustration).

Upon completion of all 12 missions on the Language Map, you will join a select group that we call our very own Language Warriors. These missions will get you in touch with a community just waiting for you. We hope you join us. It's quite the rush:

http://www.language-warriors.com/language-map

QUESTIONS FOR GROUP DISCUSSION

1. Although Nigar's story might be considered remarkable in certain aspects, how is Nigar's story similar to stories of other language learners?
2. What is your driving force, the driving reason behind learning a language?
3. What small motivators (including chocolate) seem to work on you?
4. Have you ever used summarizing, journaling, or even talking out loud as a reflection activity? Please share.

PART IV
FLEXIBILITY

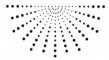

One measure of intelligence is the ability to change.

17

DAISY

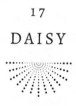

DAISY STARED AT ME, BLINKING. OBVIOUSLY, NO ONE HAD ever spoken to her that way in her life, at least not when that someone was a teacher. I had just agreed with her, giving way to her point of view. I still do not know why I did it, exactly, only that I knew that whatever teachers in the past had told her was not working. My teaching companion sat next to me with his mouth open, and Daisy's eyes, catching the full meaning of what I was saying, began to narrow. I could see a rage in her grow, like dark clouds gathering. Her fists clenched and she stood up from the table.

I had told Daisy Alvarez she was right: she probably couldn't. Some people just can't, you know. Some people aren't smart enough.

I accused Daisy Alvarez of being too dumb to read.

Let me start from the beginning, or at least a beginning. I was a young teacher serving a church mission in Venezuela. As part of my responsibilities, I would often help at schools, devising ways to support them. My companion and I would give workshops, English classes, reading lessons, and even put on cultural events, and I enjoyed meeting with schools to see what we could do. Regardless of our age and lack of experience, as enthusiastic Americans in an impoverished Venezuelan town, we were excited to serve as volunteers.

Because some of the neighborhoods where we worked were in need of reading skills, my companion and I had recently come up with a reading program. To kick off the program, we were going house to house to drop off a reading chart intended to encourage high school aged students to read an entire book. It was a challenge we felt strongly that these teenagers could do, and it is obvious to me now that even back then I enjoyed giving assignments that were big, impossible, and exciting. My companion and I went from house to house and tried to light fires in each student. We had been rather successful, and I was encouraged by the reception.

Then there was Daisy. Daisy was a 17-year old with fair skin, brown eyes, and jet-black hair. Her look was punctuated by a fierceness, a sort of I-dare-you scowl, and was accompanied by the moodiness typical of teenagers who find adults tedious and deceitful.

Deceitful is precisely how she interpreted my companion and me. We had knocked on the door, and once ushered in, we sat down with her mother, sister, and her. Once seated, we explained the program. Her younger sister seemed encouraged, took the chart from our hands with enthusiasm, and nodded repeatedly. Daisy, on the other hand, simply sat across the table from us and said nothing. It became uncomfortable. The mother left on the pretense of needing to clean the home. The younger sister suddenly had something she needed to do.

But I don't give up easily. Feeling Daisy's frostiness, I tried to tell her that I was sure she could do it. She could read the entire book within the three-week period we had assigned, and I was sure that with some effort, she would be successful. She responded with continued silence, and my companion offered words of encouragement as well. No response. It was obvious we were striking out. We shifted in our seats and I began thinking we should leave.

"You teachers always smile," she said, finally breaking the silence. "That's how I know you are lying. You smile and then say the same thing."

"What do you mean?" I asked, somewhat stunned by her directness.

"I can't do it. All the teachers tell me I am smart and that I can do it. But I can't do it. I am not smart like everyone. I am not good at reading. I'm not smart enough."

My companion interjected. He told her that was not true. Of course she was smart; it was obvious to anyone who spent any time with her. We had read with her before, and we had seen that she had enough skills to be successful. He explained that it would take effort, and that the effort would help her become better. She threw back her head and laughed.

"You're all the same. You say the same thing to every student. I don't want to join your program."

She crossed her arms and waited. Seeing that she was waiting for a response, I quickly calculated another course. I imagined her frustration at teachers who simply give false motivational speeches, who simply encourage without giving real direction or individualized attention. I saw how she must have seen us— people more interested in promoting the success of our program than with any real interest in her. I imagined years upon years of teachers telling her she could do something that she knew deep inside was something she struggled with.

Of course she felt lied to! It was obvious to me in that moment that she believed she struggled where others did not. The fact that I did not believe any of this made no difference. Her opinion was her reality. Having come upon this realization, and seeing no other options, I decided to reverse my approach.

I sighed, trying to let the exasperation seep into my voice, as if I were defeated.

"You're right."

"What?" she said.

I felt her eyes on me as if for the first time, inquisitive, unsure. I sighed again.

"You're right," I said, then threw up my hands. "Some people just can't read very well. Some people just don't have it. They can't do it. Some people just aren't smart enough."

I tried to mirror her words as closely as I could, but I could see immediately that while she was allowed to insult herself, I was under no circumstances given that same permission. I had hit a raw nerve. Her eyes turned to steel, and then to fire. I put my hands out and pretended to soften the blow.

"That's okay," I said. "Not everyone has to be a reader. Your sister took the chart; she can do it for your family. You can do other things. I am sure you can be good at a lot of other things."

She physically flinched when I mentioned her sister, and there was another pause, as if she were deciding how to respond.

"I can be good at other things?" she repeated, dumbfounded.

"Yeah. Not everyone is a reader, Daisy. You're right. Some people can't. Some people don't. Some people won't. If you want to be that person, you can. You have that choice."

The effect was as if I had just struck her in the face. Without another word, Daisy Alvarez stood up from the table, walked out of the room, and slammed a door.

Whatever effect I thought I would have on her, I now found myself alone with my companion, who turned to me sharply and said, under his breath, "What are you doing?"

I told him that I wasn't sure. I knew only that Daisy felt lied to, and that she did not see her own thinking as a choice.

With very few exceptions, learning is a choice.

YOU KNOW ENOUGH

DAISY IS FACED WITH A CHOICE. WE ALL ARE, REALLY. WE ARE faced with the choice of believing that we can or cannot. In suggesting this, I am not pretending that each of us has precisely the same journey, and some of us will undoubtedly have a harder time than others will. However, to this point in her story, I hope you will agree with me that Daisy has decided to believe in a narrative that affects her progress. In other words, the biggest thing stopping Daisy…is Daisy.

Daisy is not alone. In fact, I find it fascinating how often my learners do not recognize that their own thinking is what is getting in the way of their progress. They simply do not see their thoughts outside of reality; they think their thoughts *are* reality. Having spent years in discussions with language learners, I can tell you that learners' thoughts are quite predictable, and are generally variations of the following:

- *I can't*
- *I won't*
- *I'm different from others* (not in a positive way)

However, if Daisy (and you) can get over this first major hurdle by flipping the script, there is a sort of liberation.

- *I can*
- *I will*
- *I'm different from others* (in a positive way)

It is a freeing thing to realize that your thinking makes the biggest difference. If I were to summarize all the negative thoughts listed above into a single phrase (not to mention many other comments I have heard over the years), I would probably choose this phrase: "I am not enough." Perhaps you can hear the "I'm not enough" phrase in the following statements:

- *I'm not gifted at language like Bill.*
- *I need more vocabulary to join that dinner party.*
- *I just don't have time right now.*

This one thought—*I am not enough*—is one, as a language instructor, I have to fight against every day.

Conquering this particular kind of fear is like conquering other non-reality-based fears. A close friend of mine once revealed that he had obsessive-compulsive disorder, and that he had a particular fear of toilets. Toilets are gross. Toilets are germ infested. A public toilet is the worst possible vector of disease. His therapist's solution? To confront that fear with the worst possible scenario. The therapist suggested he lick a toilet seat. That's right. Lick a toilet seat.

Friend: How is that supposed to help me?
Therapist: Why? What do you think will happen?
Friend: I would get sick. I could get the Bubonic plague. I could die!
Therapist: Bubonic plague?

Friend: Okay, so maybe not the Bubonic plague. But I could get seriously sick. I'd be sick for a week.

Therapist: Well, if that is the worst thing that can happen, might as well get it out of the way than live in fear of it for the rest of your life.

Friend: Oh. You mean that if the worst thing that can happen happens, then...

Therapist: Then you're sick for a week. And then...

Friend: Oh, I see. And then I won't be sick. I'll be fine. I won't die.

Therapist: Okay. So now, you know the worst that can happen. How do you feel?

Friend: Good. How'd you do that?

The therapist went on to explain that when you speak the fear aloud, confront that irrational fear, then it loses its power and you can go ahead and keep on living.

Friend: Um. One more question. Do I...?

Therapist: No, you should not really lick a toilet seat.

Friend: Phew!

Let us apply this principle to language learning. As you progress in learning a language, no doubt you will encounter some fears, and with some luck, you will recognize that many of these fears are irrational. Once you identify them and confront them head on, they will lose their power.

As you confront a fear, you may want to remember my friend and ask the simple question, *What is the worst thing that can happen?* You will discover that, largely, the worst thing that can happen is mild discomfort or embarrassment.

Let me illustrate with one more story. For a number of years, I have helped recruit American teachers to teach English in Japan. When they are hired, they have several months to prepare, and almost all of them intend to learn Japanese during those months. However, life often gets in the way, and the majority of these aspiring language teachers do not study as much as they think they should. When the day finally arrives, each one lands one by one in the Narita International Airport in Tokyo. With suitcases in hand, all alone in one of the largest airports in the world, they each come to the same thoughts. *How will I ever communicate? Why didn't I study harder? Will I even make it to the hotel? Am I going to die alone on the streets of Tokyo?*

The truth is, they all make it. Every. Single. One of them. Often they will have to use their broken Japanese phrases and gestures to get by. They will have to look for familiar signs or search out someone with enough English that they can figure out their next move. With a few words, a dictionary, perhaps a friendly stranger, they make it to their hotel. They learn, as all true language explorers do, that resources from within you and resources from without show up just in time.

I illustrate this story to demonstrate to you that no matter what language level you may be at, you will be surprised to discover that—in the moment—you will be enough. You will get to your hotel, you will communicate with the right people, and you will be surprised to discover how often the universe will throw you a life preserver. You are enough.

There is no reason to delay language practice. You have all the tools necessary to be successful.

19

CHOOSING

Discovering that you are enough is an important first step. Just deciding that you can do something, conceptualizing that it is within your grasp, is a huge step. When it comes to learning a language, this kind of belief will help you as you set up a language ecosystem. However, with the choice of learning a language now decided, a new thought will occur to you.

If you are like most, the thought will look something like this: Okay, sure, so I can learn a language, but where in the world do I begin? With thousands of websites, apps, movies, and textbooks, language learning has never been easier, but it has also never been more confusing. Rather than pitch just a single product to you (which I think would be dishonest), let me help you learn how to navigate the language learning landscape with a few tips.

A particular strategy for building a language ecosystem, and one that I recommend especially in the first year of study, is a monthly theme paired with something called a "speech act."

CHOOSE A MONTHLY THEME

Teachers, textbook writers, and so-called experts often have to sort through the thousands of ways to approach language learning and come up with something coherent for their students. If you can free yourself from the idea that you do not know anything and could not possibly choose, you will realize that you CAN choose and that you know more about what you like and want than anyone else. At the very least, you can come up with themes just as well as any expert can.

I recommend that you choose a theme for an entire month (again, the Language Map chooses 12 themes for you so that you can see how this is done). Themes such as family, shopping, and hobbies can help you as you search for vocabulary, grammar activities, movies, and music. You might choose a theme based on a high- interest topic (like sports, music, and education), or based on specific language items (commands, shapes and colors, verbs).

ADD SPEECH ACTS

A way to boost your language focus when you choose a theme is to choose one or more speech acts that might fit into a particular theme. Speech acts are functional bits of language, like asking for permission, thanking, and complimenting. I often try to pair a theme—for example, making friends—to the speech act that makes most sense (introducing yourself, greeting others, complimenting). Do you know any themes or speech acts off the top of your head?

COMMON THEMES AND SPEECH ACTS IN A LANGUAGE ECOSYSTEM

General Themes

- Family
- Friends
- Shopping
- Fashion
- People
- Feelings
- Technology
- Education
- Food
- Hobbies
- Body
- Jobs
- Holidays
- Famous People
- Music
- Sports
- Falling in Love
- Having a Baby
- Children and Parenting
- Growing Old
- Vacation and Travel
- Current Events
- Humor
- Movies
- Nature Cultural Traditions
- Favorite Stories
- Favorite Things
- Time and Calendars
- Numbers
- Commands
- Colors and Shapes
- Common Verbs

- Prepositions
- Common Words
- Adverbs and Adjectives
- Phrases and Expressions

Speech Acts

- asking questions
- apologize
- describe people
- introduce self and others
- request assistance
- express needs and wants
- give and follow oral directions
- give and follow written directions
- take leave (excuse yourself)
- express satisfaction or dissatisfaction
- agree and disagree
- use the telephone
- request
- talk about sizes
- express emotions
- describe things
- describe surroundings
- describe problems
- make small talk
- give reasons and explanations
- ask for and give advice
- express thanks
- ask permission
- ask for information
- ask for and give directions
- ask for clarification
- close a conversation

- congratulate
- express anger
- express necessity
- express preference
- get attention
- give and receive compliments
- give and receive invitations
- guide a conversation
- make excuses

ONE MORE NOTE ABOUT CHOOSING

A *New York Times* article smartly titled, "The Paralyzing Problem with Too Many Choices" cites a rather famous study on, of all things, jam (Tugend, 2010). In the study, Sheena Iyengar, a researcher at Colombia University, describes how customers responded when given a choice between a display with twenty-four jams and another with just six.

What Iyengar discovered is that while more customers hovered around the display with twenty-four jams (sixty percent of all potential customers compared with forty percent), the larger selection of jams deterred people from buying. In fact, only three percent of those who stopped at the display purchased jam. When the display was limited to six jams, sales improved significantly, with thirty percent purchasing a jam.

Her conclusion: too many choices can often lead to debilitated decision-making, which ultimately leads to inaction.

DON'T GET JAMMED UP

The online world has certainly changed language learning, and even by limiting your choices by specific theme, you will likely find hundreds if not thousands of resources in your target language. The language ecosystem is impressive in its ability to provide freedom to learn in a natural, immersive way. It gives learners the power to select movies, music, speaking companions, and textbooks for themselves. In effect, it puts you in charge of your learning process, and can provide you with insights that will forever change your life.

However, simply going out into the world and randomly choosing tasks is not a viable language ecosystem. That would be a lot like having a huge selection of jams to choose from, but no direction on which one works best for you. A good language ecosystem will not only give you keen insight on all the possibilities (movies, games, strategies, and so forth), but also how to limit those possibilities in order to achieve your best outcome.

START NOTICING PRIORITIES

To further help you narrow your choices (from 24 to 6) let us discuss priorities. Remember that it is not just "doing a lot of language stuff" that will bring you success (remember how hard Gouin worked), rather that there are some tasks that are simply better than others are. Learning to prioritize these tasks becomes key. Let us talk about how to prioritize in the next few chapters by using the metaphor of a canning jar.

Choose a monthly theme and build tasks around it.

20

PRIORITIZING

STEPHEN R. COVEY (2017) ONCE EXPLAINED THE IMPORTANCE of priorities by using an experience he had in a business class. He stated that a professor stood in front of a group of students and set a large canning jar in front of them. He filled it to the top with rocks and asked the students if it was full. They responded yes. Then he took out a bucket of sand and filled the jar again, and students watched as the sand poured inside the spaces between the large rocks. The professor asked again if the jar was full. This time students hesitated, and with good reason. The professor proceeded to fill the jar with a pitcher of water, after which he asked the students to explain the purpose behind this visual demonstration. After several incorrect responses, (including something along the lines of, *There is always room for more stuff in your life*), the professor gave his answer, which amounts to this: Unless you put the rocks in first, they will never fit into the jar.

This story demonstrates the principle of prioritizing, of knowing what matters most and what matters least, and that what matters most must be placed in the first position. No doubt, this is a very relevant way to analyze your own ecosystem.

As you move forward in developing a lifestyle that incorporates language learning, you must constantly reflect on whether or not you have prioritized your tasks well. If you imagine your ecosystem as the canning jar, and your language tasks as items that fill up the jar, you can see how making the right decisions will increase your chances of not only enjoying the learning process but making it more successful.

Always remember that it is not just "doing a lot of language stuff" that will bring you success (remember how hard Gouin worked) but rather that by putting priorities in their place, language learning can happen on its own.

Let's talk about how to prioritize language learning tasks by using the metaphor of the canning jar itself and discuss two concepts: fixed and fluid.

DEFINING FIXED AND FLUID

By fixed, I refer to the idea that some tasks are more consequential than others are. The best of these (think of the rocks in the canning jar) are more essential and, as a result, should be more permanent. Often, these tasks are the most beneficial to language outcomes. I sometimes refer to these as your "bread and butter" tasks, meaning that they are a staple of your language ecosystem.

Conversely, there are tasks that are not nearly as consequential but may be a lot more fun. These tasks are more liquid (think of the water in the canning jar), by which I mean that they are not nearly as permanent. They are fluid and subject to change from week to week, and often represent tasks that keep things exciting.

CHOOSING FIXED (BREAD AND BUTTER) TASKS

Now let me share some personal examples of my fixed and fluid tasks. For my fixed, or bread-and-butter, tasks, I usually try to choose things I naturally do anyway. In other words, it is important to choose times and tasks that already mirror your current lifestyle and schedule.

A language ecosystem is best accomplished when things are a natural extension of you. For this reason, I choose to read about fifteen minutes of a foreign language every morning because it is a habit I have had since I was young. As an avid Christian from a strong Christian family, I have a habit of waking up, grabbing my phone, and reading from the Holy Scriptures. I have them available in English if I get stuck, but I love to move back and forth between the languages that I am continually learning (French, Spanish, and Portuguese).

Again, this activity is a bread and butter activity because it is daily, because it is a permanent fixture in my life already, and because it is something that I know brings me direct, daily exposure to the language. To support this major activity, however, I have a number of minor strategies that help to supplement it, including:

- Relying on an online dictionary for unknown words
- A verb conjugator app to help me practice verbs I do not recognize
- A notebook filled with sentences and phrases I am learning
- A journal that gives me a chance to summarize (in the target language) what I just read

Another bread-and-butter task that I do almost every day is listen to a podcast on my daily commute to work. I love listening to podcasts or the radio, so again, this is something I do as a matter of routine and feels quite natural to me. For French, I listen to *Le Journal en Français Facile*. In Spanish, I listen to *ESPN deportes* (I am a sports junkie), and for Portuguese I have a podcast that I listen to called *Radio Japan Podcasting NHK World*

Portuguese. Since I have a thirty-minute drive, I usually am able to listen to the French every day (it is 15 minutes) and then alternate between Spanish and Portuguese according to my mood.

Again, I truly enjoy these tasks and they are natural extensions of who I am already, so if this sounds like drudgery, then you will have to think of tasks that fit your particular lifestyle. I am just a naturally inquisitive talk radio kind of guy, and the point is to find something that approximates who you are.

CHOOSING FLUID TASKS

Having a daily study routine of bread and butter tasks is key, but that does not mean that the fluid tasks are less important. The fluid tasks are essential to keep up your desire to learn a language. Fluid tasks are flexible, involve a lot of searching and discovering, and will lead you on adventures to find something that you truly enjoy.

Let me get back to specifics in my own case. When I have a few minutes to myself, I often search for new releases of movies I can find in French, Spanish, or Portuguese (among others). Recently I finished a series called *Três Por Cento*, a Brazilian thriller about a dystopian future. It was something I enjoyed doing whenever I found the time. I also found some of my favorite movies in Spanish or French, and sometimes I will watch one of them. In other words, these activities are variable, and depend on my mood and situation.

Therefore, while a fixed activity is a proven, durable activity, fluid tasks are, above all, flexible. Some of them I really get into, but others never really grab me, and I spend a lot of time searching and exploring multiple options. I look up music and short movies on YouTube channels, Netflix, or Amazon Prime. I explore interesting articles from online newspapers or watch Ted Talks in the language of my choice. I might spend time on a phone app or look up tasks on language websites and print them out. Here is where I am the most adventurous, the most unattached to a particular program or textbook. I simply look for stuff that interests me.

That does not mean that I do not try to learn while I am in this "explore" mode. If I am feeling serious, I often bring a notebook, summarize, or do any of the other tasks I do with my bread-and-butter tasks. However, the main point of these tasks is to continue my motivation and joy for the cultures and languages I am trying to learn, and I like to find things that inspire that feeling in me.

ENTRY POINTS

Another way to think of fluid tasks is to discuss them as entry points into the language environment. An entry point is an exciting, motivating lens into a culture, one that drives you to learn more about it. I cannot tell you how often I have heard the story of the language learner who never thought of learning a language until something grabbed him or her.

For a friend from Brazil that I met just today named Samuel, it was Bob Marley that caused a spark. At age 12, he fell in love with Bob Marley's music and, curious to understand the meaning behind the words he was beginning to recognize, he began to look up lyrics. This became an entry point—a hook, if you will—that would later grow.

I had a wonderful conversation with another friend. Her name is Sash, and she is from Russia. She told me that she has traveled and lived in two different countries (the U.S. and in Japan). While she learned English during her time in the states, she was curious why she had never picked up Japanese, so we spent a part of the evening discussing why. What we came upon was that, while she immersed herself in both situations, immersion was not enough. Like Samuel, with English she had clear entry points that drove her toward English; whereas in Japan, she worked mostly with foreigners. Working with foreigners (who mostly spoke English) prevented her from entering completely into a Japanese language environment.

BALANCING FIXED AND FLUID

As you consider adding items to your ecosystem, make sure you have a foundation of fixed and fluid tasks. As you do so, keep in mind that you are constantly searching for the right balance. Because balance is the goal, you will constantly want to approach each task with flexibility. You may find that one activity that you thought was only for fun becomes a major portion of your study, and you may want to "grant" it fixed status, whereas some things that you thought were permanent have worn out their welcome and are demoted to "fluid."

Find both fixed and fluid tasks that work for you.

LIFE PRESERVER STRATEGIES

No matter how well you choose or how well you prioritize, eventually you will find yourself treading in deep water. Language learning just does that to you.

In Venezuela, for example, at one point I was assigned to answer phones in an office. One day, a man called and after a brief conversation, he became so irate he told me several times to hang up the phone. He had a thick accent and quick, pulsating way of speaking, and although I tried to reply, I simply did not understand. To add to his frustration, even though I had spent an entire year in Venezuela, I had never heard the verb *hang up*. So, to each request, I simply said, "I'm sorry. I don't understand." And each time he had to explain, his frustration grew. He yelled at me, told me how obtuse I was, called me a name I'd rather not repeat, and then *he* hung up. (As a side note, I never forgot the word after that day: the verb is *colgar*.)

I was embarrassed, felt like a failure at my job, and for weeks I was worried that he would call back—or worse, show up at our office. Of course, the truth is, I did not contract the Bubonic plague, and I did not die. After all, it was just embarrassment.

However, it still stung, and I remember wishing that I could have done a better job at communicating with him.

When you find yourself in a tough position, yes, you may indeed face some embarrassment. However, there are strategies you can use, strategies that I wish I had known at that young age, that will help you navigate these deeper waters. In fact, when facing difficult situations, these techniques will increase your ability to be more flexible. I call these *Life Preserver Strategies*.

HEDGING AND REPAIRING

Hedging and repairing are twin techniques that allow you to help others know you are struggling. Hedging means that you are expressing uncertainty, which you can do by using gestures like shrugging your shoulders, pausing, and wrinkling your forehead. Phrases such as *I'm not certain I'm saying this correctly* or *I don't speak very well* also invite a listener to help you.

Equally important is the skill of repairing, which involves a number of phrases that invite a listener to help you fix something you said incorrectly. Phrases such as *I'm looking for a word* or *I can't say this well. I think the word is…* will allow people who don't understand you to change their attitude. Instead of being angry with you, most listeners will attempt to join you in your efforts. This will turn them from opponents into supporters.

Learning how to hedge and repair will make you a better communicator and make you less fearful of times when you simply don't have the words to say. Make sure you study the worksheet in the back for specific ways to improve these twin strategies.

RECOMBINATION

Recombination is a fancy term that means "to say things in a different way." In other words, often as you are writing or speaking, you may run into the problem of not finding the right word, or not having the word at all.

Recombination is a skill that invites people to use the words they know to explain something they do not know. When you find that someone does not understand you, rather than just continually repeating the word, try a different way of saying it. It can be fun to figure out different ways to say the same thing.

At one recent conference, for example, scientists were invited to use only the most common 1,000 words in English to share their research. At a recent Ecological Society of America (Atkins, 2016), researchers that usually used terms such as *greenhouse* and *nitrogen deposition* had to find a different way to express these same ideas (*greenhouse* became "hot box," and *nitrogen deposition* became "extra ground food to make green things for humans"). My favorite was *X-ray*, which became the "special machine that doctors use to look inside of you." Indeed.

CULLING FOR ANSWERS

Once again, imagine that you are in a situation where you do not know the answer. Hedging and repairing are strategies that invite others to join you in finding an answer, and recombination is a way of finding an answer within yourself. Culling for answers is the strategy to use when the other two strategies fail.

Culling means searching but searching in a flexible way. If you do not find an answer in yourself, among your friends, or in a dictionary, then you keep looking through the resources you have created. This strategy means that you can patiently and methodically keep looking without getting discouraged. The online world, again, has opened our minds to these possibilities in our daily lives.

When my wife does not know the answer to a particular question, she often posts a question on social media, looks through online forums, or searches for YouTube videos. Good language learners do not stop when they do not know an answer; they go find it.

GRIT AND GOAL SETTING

So, what happened with Daisy Alvarez? Let me explain. Two days after our unfortunate meeting, my companion and I were walking near the school when a girl approached us: it was Daisy's kid sister. She came at us in a full sprint, and when I realized who it was, my heart leapt. I braced for the worst and expected her to yell at me.

"What did you do to my sister?" she said.

I groaned inside. This was going to be bad. She asked again when I did not reply.

"What did you do to my sister?"

I tried to read this young girl's face, and I couldn't. I stammered and said that we were trying the best we could to get her to read. I looked over at my companion, who was shrugging his shoulders. Expecting to hear Daisy's sister tell me I was a horrible person, I was surprised to see her face soften. She then said something I found totally unexpected.

"She hasn't stopped reading for two days."

"What?" I said, incredulously.

"Daisy. She hasn't stopped reading for two days. She keeps going back to her room and muttering your name."

"Muttering my name?"

"Yes. She reads for hours, comes out of her room and says, 'Thinks I can't read? I'll show him I can read. How dare he!'"

"You mean she's reading? You mean, it worked?"

"Worked? What worked? Seriously…what did you do to my sister?" Daisy's sister's eyes filled with tears, and I could see her smile. "She has never wanted to read. Don't you know what you have done? My parents are so happy. My sister is doing something she has never done before. Daisy is reading!"

My body relaxed. I had not realized how tense I had been for the last two days. For two days I had imagined different scenarios where Daisy, or her mother, or another family member approached me with anger and malice (and possibly a baseball bat). This, on the other hand, was the best news I could have received. Daisy's sister thanked me again and told me that her parents had invited us over for dinner later that week. I was thrilled.

It occurs to me that, at least that day, I never really answered Daisy's sister. The truth is, I didn't know what to say, and I still wasn't sure what I had done to cause that kind of change. I had only felt that to keep smiling at her and telling her she was smart would come off wrong, and that a change in tactic was necessary. Now, with the advantage of years to reflect on this incident, I have come to at least a couple of conclusions.

The first is that when we are failing at something, it is important for us to try something else. No doubt that a change of pace, a change of style, a change of direction can do us all good. Flexibility, the subject matter of these last few chapters, is a key to progression.

The second is a little more subtle. I think that my exchange with Daisy did not really give her any special power or ability; rather it revealed something she had inside her all along. While I certainly do not recommend that teachers use reverse psychology at the risk of having students hate you, in this instance, by making myself her enemy, I gave her a goal. Her goal was to prove Shane Dixon wrong.

As we finish this particular section, I would like to remind each of you language learners that you have everything inside of you that is necessary to be successful. However, it is your grit and your determination spurred on by a goal that will often give you the courage to overcome challenges. To obtain that kind of grit, if you require me to come over to your house and call you a loser with no hope of accomplishing such goals, please just let me know.

Use life preserver strategies when you find yourself in potentially deep waters.

∼

QUESTIONS FOR GROUP DISCUSSION

1. What does Daisy's story tell us about language learning? Do you sometimes stop your own progress? What do you do to "get over" yourself?
2. How does the canning jar example apply in your life? What priorities do you have for yourself? How do you assess those priorities?
3. Can you imagine getting into hot water while learning a language? What strategies attract you the most based on the kinds of situations you think you will run into?

PART V
DETAILS

I am always doing what I can't do yet in order to learn how to do it.

— VINCENT VAN GOGH

THE ASSUMPTION OF EQUIVALENCY

In 2011, I decided to pursue a Ph.D. With the ecosystem concept clearly in mind, I realized that online education would become increasingly important to language learning. As individuals began to accept that immersion could happen anywhere through the use of technology, educators would need to learn teaching—and learning—online.

After researching some of the best university programs, I was happy to discover that a top ten program existed within my own university. Even more compelling, because the program had classes that were held in the evenings, I would be able to continue my employment (which felt important because, apparently, my children still wanted to eat every day).

After discussing the option with my wife, I applied. Then I waited. A short time later, I was accepted to the educational technology program at Arizona State University where, unsurprisingly, several of the classes were held exclusively online.

One such class was called the "Impact of Emerging Technologies." I was quite excited to learn about both the good and bad of online learning—its advantages and the problems that would naturally come with it.

Advantages to online learning were obvious to me: people could take courses from long-distance, and often, through online discussion boards, could have the freedom to discuss ideas whenever they wanted. This creates opportunities for people all over the world to form educational communities, and people who traditionally could not get access to high quality education could now do so. All of this excited me.

However, I was still skeptical in several regards. For one thing, I had seen firsthand how online education still lagged far behind in certain aspects. Many professors, for example, assumed that lectures in a classroom needed only to be uploaded (with an accompanying PowerPoint presentation) and that this was assumed to be sufficiently similar to an in-class experience.

In addition, classroom participation was often limited online, consisting of discussion boards and chat rooms with very little teacher supervision or correction, meaning that difficult concepts that needed a teacher's input were often ignored. In fact, I had seen firsthand how discussion boards often became unthoughtful responses to readings, with students playing the game of responding to others in the most blasé manner imaginable. In short, we weren't thinking, we were doing just enough to appear like we were thinking so that we could get points.

On one such occasion and in the class I just mentioned, the irony of bad online design while learning about online design became too much for me.

My professor posted an article on online education and asked each member of the class to do two things: respond to the article, and then respond to two other students' responses. As I read the article, it became obvious that it was a lightly researched piece with handpicked studies that showed that online education was wonderful, and in fact, equivalent or better than face-to-face instruction. One study, in particular, suggested that because every student got to speak online, that this equated to rich, complex discussions that could never be had in a classroom. The irony was that, in the discussion board we were required to respond to, I saw each student simply agree with the article, and then post a single sentence in response to a fellow classmate. To me, it was obvious that none of us were thinking critically.

When thinking of the comment I wanted to post, I found that I simply couldn't agree with the article or with my fellow students' response to it. While I maintained a sense of decorum and never attacked the students outright, I wrote a lengthy comment mentioning other studies, studies that demonstrated that online education had shown clear signs of increased cheating, lower levels of engagement, and added frustration among technophobic learners. I stated that I was a fan of online education, but my desire to join the online educational world was not simply to think in terms of its benefits, but to make it better than it was.

Unsurprisingly, at least one student complained about my post, thinking that I was a rabble-rouser trying to stir the online pot. I had, after all, called students out on the game they were playing. My intent, however, was not to cause problems, but to encourage thought. However, not knowing my intent or tone (which can be another problem with online forums), the teacher made an appointment to see me and quell any online rebellion I was attempting to create. I agreed to meet with her.

She was a thoughtful professor, and as we spoke, I believe she saw that the intent was to have an actual discussion: to discuss not only the possibilities that online education represented, but also the ways we could and should shape it. She agreed that online class discussions often devolved into acritical thought, and she welcomed me to continue. However, by the end, I sensed that she was still unhappy that I had challenged the assignment, and that it would have been better (and easier) if I had just been willing to play the game the other students played.

This experience taught me at least two things. First, I learned a bit about myself. I wasn't simply entering the online educational world to be a part of it; rather, I wanted to challenge it and make it better. I had a healthy dose of discontent, and I felt certain that current models could be improved. Second, I realized that challenging the status quo, as I had done earlier with national language plans, is often met with resistance, even if what I am challenging accurately depicts the educational landscape.

Education, such as the kind common to online education, must be more than just getting exposed to the information a classroom teacher throws up on the internet, and it must help learners become better at self-directed learning. In other words, how do you help learners learn how to learn?

This concern is much greater than just how long a video should be, or the types of assessment questions you put online. This concern demonstrates an understanding that learners, since they are now without the help of a teacher or guide, must assume more responsibility and pay attention to details they otherwise would never have noticed.

This is perhaps even truer for someone learning a language online. Because online language learning is such a shift from classroom language learning, a new set of tools and careful attention to certain details is a necessity. In fact, I have noticed that an ecosystem that does not pay attention to these details is not an ecosystem at all.

Self-directed online language learning is a new kind of learning, and a specific set of tools is required.

23

WHO LEARNS BETTER?

As a language-learning expert, one of the questions I am most often asked is this: who learns better, children or adults? Many people assume that children, because of their greater brain plasticity, ability to master sounds, and faster recall, are by far the better language learners (and yes, all three of the mentioned items give children an edge). I have also heard the assumption that women, because of small neurological differences (the right and left hemispheres are slightly more connected, for example), are also superior language learners. In fact, there are a whole string of assumptions that language non-professionals (and professionals) regularly share. Here are a few more:

- Extroverts learn language better than introverts
- "Right brain" learners (intuitive) have an advantage to "left brain" (mathematical) learners
- Those who focus on meaning learn better than those who focus on grammar

Over the years I have noticed a number of pairings that are

similar, and while each pairing is not precisely the same, there is almost always an assumption that favors a particular learner or learning style over another. In the graphic below, I have placed the "superior" style (or the style assumed by a member of a group) in the left column, and the "inferior" style in the right.

Assumed Superior	Assumed Inferior
Focus on Meaning	Focus on Form
Right Brain	Left Brain
Top-Down Processing	Bottom-Up Processing
Children	Adults
Diffuse	Focused
Relaxed	Determined
Extroverts	Introverts
Women	Men

When I am asked to make a distinction like the ones shown previously, I am rarely asked the advantages and/or disadvantages of each learning style. Rather, what I am being asked is to side with one learner style or group over another.

If I'm not careful, I, like many of my professional counterparts, will choose the left column. By doing so, I overlook the complexity of the issue, and can discount advantages inherent to the "inferior" style. So why would I ever do this?

As I have thought about this common trend, I have concluded that it is human nature to prefer a winner and a loser. By proclaiming winners, we can maintain a sort of intellectual laziness, the kind that allows us to dismiss adults, introverts, even members of an entire gender as poor language learners. *Well, that must be the reason I can't learn a language,* someone might reason. *I'm too old/too shy/too male.* By providing people one-sided answers that support these phrases—which amount to nothing more than rationalizations—academics are supplying people with justifications for not growing.

The truth about these pairings is a bit stickier, but far more interesting. The "inferior" styles found in the right column of the graphic end up providing valuable knowledge of how to learn a language, and the "superior" styles present potential pitfalls.

To demonstrate, let me tell you a story of two groups of students I once had: Italian and Japanese executives. As I share this story, I want to be clear that I am not suggesting all Italians or Japanese are like the two groups in question, only that these two specific groups represented two different styles common to language learning.

One summer I taught a group of Italian directors. They were an affluent, charming, well-dressed group of extroverts, with an insatiable desire to improve their English and communicate. Although they had arrived in the U.S. to improve their business English skills, it became apparent that these professionals were willing to talk about, well, just about anything. In stereotypical Italian fashion, they spoke with their hands, engaging quickly in numerous conversations about family and friends, politics, dating, marriage, and any other number of high interest topics. They enjoyed giving oral presentations and nearly every speaking task I gave them.

At about the same time, I received a group of Japanese business professionals also looking to improve their business English. The contrast could not have been more obvious. These executives rarely spoke outside of the business context, and typically responded to a question only when called upon. They worked almost exclusively from the class material and textbooks, taking notes on every grammatical form I put on the board, but then showing very little interest in using and practicing the forms given. They particularly enjoyed writing down dialogues and memorizing them, struggling to create their own language forms and relying heavily on the forms I provided.

So, who were the better learners? The graphic I previously shared would definitely point to the Italian group as the superior learners. They, after all, were answering questions in class, engaging in oral performance, and could not help but talk each day. In other words, they focused on meaning not form, they used top down processes, a more diffuse, creative approach to language learning, and were not averse to risk. As one of my fellow teachers said in jest, "Why would the Italians let something as small as English stop them from speaking?"

In contrast, the Japanese executives struggled to speak in groups and generate the same amount of conversation as the Italians. The richness of the discussions was somewhat limited by constant pauses caused by a fear of making errors. While they were studious and conscientious, they were also much less willing to get outside their comfort zone and make mistakes. So, who performed better when it came to results? Here is where it gets interesting.

Unsurprisingly, the Italians received their highest marks in speaking ability, usually exceeding their counterparts in oral fluency and ability to communicate a message. They also outperformed informal measures such as how teachers felt about them. Teachers consistently noted how "language friendly" the Italians were in terms of their ability to engage in course material. In some sense, the Italians had met or exceeded American expectations of what a good language learner looks like. They were engaged. They were willing. They were speaking up and speaking out.

Nevertheless, some unusual evidence also presented itself that told me to be cautious before declaring the Italian group clear-cut winners. Several trends clearly pointed to the fact that the Japanese group had begun to outgain the Italian group in certain linguistic areas.

First of all, although they had scored similarly in an entrance exam, by the end of the course the Japanese businessmen had higher scores than their counterparts in written examinations, listening comprehension quizzes, reading comprehension tests, and pretty much any and every other measure I threw at them. While their ability to speak was perhaps more limited than that of the Italian executives, even in speaking there was progress that I did not expect.

What I noticed was that, when given a chance to "re-perform," meaning to give the same exact presentation after receiving feedback, the Japanese executives were by far the superior group. They took my notes seriously, wrote down each phrase I asked them to work on, and came back and performed better the second time. In contrast, I saw a clear difference in how the Italian executives received feedback. They treated the feedback a bit more loosely, rarely taking my advice from one presentation into the next, instead constantly focusing on the messages they wanted to share.

What this and other experiences have taught me is to be cautious of assigning winners and losers to the language game. Furthermore, while risk, exploration, and willingness to make mistakes are all useful to the language learning process, there is another mode of learning that is essential, and it is found in the right side, not the left side, of the column.

A key to language learning is the ability to pay attention to feedback and make small adjustments.

24

SWITCH IT UP

IN THE LAST CHAPTER, I USED A PERSONAL EXPERIENCE TO suggest that assigning winners and losers to the language game leaves strengths and weaknesses of each approach unexamined. Now let us examine two approaches in terms of the specific advantages and disadvantages within them.

I do this primarily because much of the book so far has discussed the advantages of exploring, adventure, and risk, all advantages generally found in the first list. Reasons for starting the book with these skills is that they match so well with the best language learner strategies from some of the best learners in the world.

Furthermore, most adults, as we discussed with Francois Gouin, are in need of learning to let go of the classroom-type techniques typically found in the second list.

However, a complete training regimen should include the benefits found in both learning styles, and this entire section is devoted to helping you consider the benefits of what might be called a more detail-oriented approach.

By now, the advantages of the Italian group should seem

rather obvious to you, and you may notice that much of what I have discussed in this book matches up to their learning style. Language learning, as the Italian group understood, requires learners to develop these skills:

LIST 1

- Make and keep friends (Section 1)
- Practice immediately (Section 1)
- Explore (Section 2)
- Risk looking foolish (Section 2)
- Go on language missions (Section 3)
- Choose your own topics and goals (Section 4)

These advantages were certainly prevalent among the Italian executives, and it no doubt helped them to achieve advanced speaking proficiency. They were fearless. They were fun. I was so impressed with their constant attention toward their goals and what they wanted to achieve. Their motivation was inspiring to me.

However, the advantages among my second group of executives are also worthy of consideration. While perhaps to a lesser degree, this group demonstrates skills I have mentioned throughout the book so far. For one thing, while it might appear that the Japanese students were not practicing with the forms I gave them, a closer look revealed that much of the time they spent pouring over notes, even though they were silent, involved a sort of deep internalizing of the content given, something I mention in the first section of the book. They also follow a number of other skills, including these:

LIST 2

- Predicting, preparing, and performing (Section 2)
- Monitoring their own language forms (Section 3)
- Journaling and notetaking (Section 3)
- Following fixed language tasks as assigned by the teacher (Section 4)

In short, the members of this particular group were meticulous in their ability to follow through with assignments, to predict what teachers wanted, and showed greater ability to follow through with feedback because of their constant attention to detail.

Now let's talk about the disadvantages of each style. The Italian group, in their excitement to share their ideas and be creative in expressing those ideas, often lost the original intent of certain assignments, especially specific language objectives, and thus were a bit harder to corral, so to speak. Their dedication to focusing on their ideas meant that they were often less able or willing to adapt to those ideas, which led to less improvement from one performance to another.

Perhaps the simplest way I can explain it is this: the Italian group made WAY more mistakes than the Japanese group and didn't realize or care that the mistakes were being made, as long as the message was communicated. Is that an advantage? Yes, in some ways. A disadvantage? Well, that too.

In contrast, the Japanese group, as a whole, was less willing to speak, but much more likely to get things right. This is likely why they scored higher on so many of our language assessments. They were paying attention to what we, as teachers, were asking them to do on the tests. However, here again, we see that there is an inherent disadvantage.

Perhaps the easiest way to explain this disadvantage was that sometimes the Japanese group never spoke English at lunch. While this may seem like a minor concern, it demonstrated a lack of putting into practice the very skills they were learning. In other words, sometimes they were so concerned about classroom performance that they did not translate their practice to functional performance, meaning performance in the real world and in real time…like speaking English during break times and over lunch.

So there are two main styles, and both exhibit advantages and disadvantages. Now what? There is no doubt that being like the Italian executives, with their desire to share and communicate, willingness to risk, and ability to convey and focus on meaning will be an advantage to you. However, you may find that you relate more to our Japanese executives, in which case, there are many attributes and strategies that can help you be a success. Having a primary style or disposition can certainly allow you the comfort to learn in your own way and in your own time and is something that you should feel good about.

However, while I do not recommend having you abandon your primary adult style, it is most certainly important to shore it up, or at least add to it. In other words, if you find that you are naturally a Japanese executive kind of learner, it is time for you to embrace your inner Italian. If you happen to enjoy the Italian executive way of learning a language—well, then, it is time for you to consider becoming Japanese.

No matter what your style, investigating the advantage of an alternate style will shore up your weaknesses.

25

THE RIGHT SIDE OF THE COLUMN

THE LAST CHAPTER ARGUES THAT THOSE WHO APPROACH language like my Italian executives should discover techniques found among my Japanese executives, and vice versa. It suggests that switching up your style, or at the least adding to it, is an important part of language learning.

Here is a simple graphic to display this idea visually.

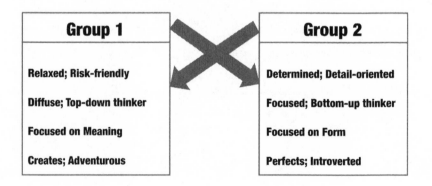

This visual expresses two primary modes of learning, and

suggests that people often fall categorically into one or the other category. The arrows represent the need for learners to inform their own style with the style of the other, rather than assuming one style is exclusive to the other.

Again, since this is a theoretical construct, it does not imply that real people are only in one category or another, rather, it is intended only to illustrate key truths. For example, rather than siding with one viewpoint or another when asked the question *Who learns best, children or adults?*, we can answer the question more completely by suggesting the fuller picture. Let us do so now.

While most professional linguists agree that children possess certain advantages, very few would suggest they possess all of the advantages. Introducing language while children are young seems like the wisest course of action, but that is not to suggest that learning at a later age does not have some built-in benefits. Included in those benefits is your tremendous knowledge of the world, and of how it works.

For example, you more easily understand complex, abstract concepts. You also have greater knowledge of popular culture and can rely on it in order to interpret the world. Finally, you have learned to navigate through the world by means of your career choices, familial responsibilities, and day-to-day management of life affairs.

In other words, you are pretty smart compared to a normal kid, and that kind of smarts can pay out in significant ways when it comes to learning a language. In fact, many of the other items in the "right" column might explain some of the advantages you have over children. Let us share a few more.

OLDER LEARNERS AND POSITIVE TRANSFER

Language transfer refers to your ability to transfer your knowledge or ability in one language to another. Take, among other things, the fact that you know a LOT of words compared to children. This gives you the ability to recognize terms and ideas in one language, and transfer them to the next. Children simply lack the knowledge base to be able to transfer, and are at a decided disadvantage when it comes to learning vocabulary and general knowledge.

DETAIL-ORIENTED LEARNERS AND BOTTOM-UP PROCESSING

Here is a skill that you might associate with Francois Gouin and his "vocabulary-collecting ways." It is called *bottom-up processing*. Bottom-up processing refers to how people with no knowledge of something new (a new word, for example) will try to understand it based on what they can perceive (let's say the definition is provided in their language). Given just a little data, these learners will quickly come to conclusions about it that "make sense," even if they are imperfect.

For example, if I told a student that *sensei* in Japanese means *teacher* in English, a bottom-up processing exercise might simply stop there. Is this a useful way to learn? Well, yes, mostly. As it turns out, the best translation for *sensei* is *teacher*. However, those who have lived in Japan are quick to note that it means much more. They note that not only is the word *sensei* more positive than the English preferred translation, but *sensei* is also used more broadly, extending to parents, bosses, and mentors. In other words, bottom-up processing in language can get you only so far in terms of understanding, but it will get you close.

Thus, the skills of bottom-up and top-down processing together are most powerful, and learners that use both are invariably more successful. Yet it should be noted that in terms of acquiring language, bottom-up learners are particularly good at paying attention to details, gathering data unattached to any real context, and memorizing individual letters, words, and sounds. They do this in order to build a foundation, one that allows them to feel comfortable exploring or risking. These souls are those who do their Duolingo or Rosetta Stone daily. They are the memorizers; and memorizing is a terrific skill.

DETAIL-ORIENTED LEARNERS AND A FOCUS ON FORM

Grammar. While for many the very word is anxiety inducing, that does not mean it is not a useful part of language learning. Children, of course, do not rely on grammatical forms to learn their first language, and often ignore rules when given a second language in home contexts.

However, when it comes to adults who have that ability to grasp abstract concepts more readily, grammatical forms can create greater language learner awareness. While it is true that a reliance on grammatical forms is often a substitute for real functional use of the language, studying grammatical forms can help adults know what to say and how to say it.

DETAIL-ORIENTED LEARNERS AND FEEDBACK

Related to the topic of focusing on forms is the notion of corrective feedback. Notice that the Italian executives plateaued in their language forms while speaking aloud, making many errors but never fixing them. Although speaking aloud is no doubt an important part of a language learning process, if you speak aloud and ignore or dismiss corrections, you miss out on the kind of steady perfecting that comes from constantly reviewing what you produce.

While some theorists worry that constant focus (or monitoring) of your speech can create undue pressure and a loss of motivation, there have to be some times when you allow yourself to review and improve.

This leads to yet another discussion. If you are sometimes

supposed to relax and ignore your mistakes, and yet at other times get focused and pay attention to errors, then when should you learn to relax, and when should you let yourself be detail-oriented? In essence, when should you focus on form, and when should you just let things flow?

Here are a few tips to manage the process of switching between one mode and another:

Tip 1: Be focused before and after.

What this tip means is that conversations, oral communication, should flow, and it is important to relax and focus on the message rather than every single detail. You simply do not want to be so in your head when you speak that you cannot get anything out at all. Thus, one thing you can do is to make sure that you focus on your speaking performances before and after.

In other words, like the Japanese executives demonstrated, prepare deeply, look carefully at your grammar, vocabulary, and pronunciation. Afterward, pay attention to what listeners say about your performance. If you have the luxury of recording your performances, you should listen carefully and pay attention to areas that need improving.

Tip 2: Be detailed in short bursts.

Gathering information, working on grammatical forms, and doing online exercises can supplement a language plan by providing clear and precise information. While I recommend a loose approach to which forms to work on, I do recommend working on forms as part of your normal regimen. In the next chapter, we will talk about how to do that using the masterful technique of the Pomodoro.

Tip 3: Be detailed when a detail fails you.

Often when communication breaks down, you will notice a particular form or detail that escaped your understanding. These moments can be embarrassing, but can provide strong evidence that you need to work on a particular form.

While giving my first speech in Spanish in front of an audience of about 100 people, I remember afterward someone telling me that I had used the wrong article for the word *tema* (which means *theme*). I had assumed that *tema*, since it ended in *a*, would be preceded with the article *la*, and so I said *la tema* in my speech. Sadly, I said it multiple times, and it bothered one rather forward listener enough to come up to me afterward and tell me so. I was embarrassed, but went home and started studying why the rule for *tema* was different from other words, and this allowed me to understand a form I had not understood entirely until that point.

Tip #4: Creation demands letting go, and perfection demands detail.

For my final tip, let me suggest that different kinds of mental processes require different modes of thinking. While we will discuss this concept more in the next section, one way to assess which mode of learning to use is to consider what kind of task you are performing. If you are asked to create something new, something creative, and something entirely unfamiliar, it is often best to employ what we call a "diffuse mode" of language learning, meaning that you allow your mind to think freely, and making connections wherever they may.

However, when you are seeking to improve or perfect a task, when the task itself involves an attempt to fill out what you already know, to grasp difficult concepts through study, then a focused mode of learning may be most appropriate.

We will discuss these two modes in detail in the next section, but for now, if you can simply remember that greater creativity requires greater relaxation, and greater improvement requires greater focus, you are on your way.

> *Engaging in a "focused mode" of learning should happen in quick bursts or when the task requires perfection.*

THE DRIVER'S SEAT

Never in the history of the world has there been so much information available. You are in the driver's seat. You can learn a language in a way that perhaps was not nearly as likely even 20 years ago. It is unbelievable what you can find on the internet: good, bad, and blah. This fact should demonstrate to you a clear opportunity and, of course, some possible dangers. The ability to teach yourself just about anything is greater than ever, however, there is so much information, that you may not know where or how to begin.

To maximize your results, any ecosystem builder will need to know self-directed learning principles and basic features of good online educational models.

PRINCIPLES OF SELF-DIRECTED LEARNING

One thing to note about the ever-growing number of courses online is how many begin a course, and how few people finish. In the massive open online course world, with large platforms that serve millions of people (Coursera, Lynda.com, EdX, and

Udemy), it is typical for a course to have a completion rate of less than four percent.

Reasons for this vary, but MOOC providers are trying to fight back with better analytics, identifying the exact video lecture or quiz that "stops" the majority of learners from progressing. This gathering of big data has allowed the MOOC world to come up with a formula of best practices, including the length of videos, the difficulty level of quizzes, the correct amount of online discussion, and so forth.

Another trend, however, is becoming obvious in the online world, and this has very little to do with the design that online educators are employing. Learners themselves have to become better consumers of information by employing techniques that will allow them to complete a course without a teacher looking over their shoulder.

Rather than the motivation caused by grades, peer pressure, and a school environment, motivation itself has shifted and narrowed. Learners are finding that motivation declines dramatically when there is no final goal, no particular achievement to hang your hat on.

Thus, online language learning requires setting specific goals, and then finding ways to incentivize each achievement, often with a massive reward at the end that drives learners on to completion.

Self-directed learning also requires a shift in power dynamics. Rather than having a teacher control the classroom content and objectives, learners themselves are given more control over their environment, and this means that they must now manage the load that was typically placed onto the shoulders of teachers. For example, in addition to setting goals for themselves, learners need to think about:

- curriculum pace—how much each day and each week
- curriculum design—what works and what doesn't
- curriculum assessment—how do I know if this is working or not?

In these ways, online language learners now assume roles traditionally assumed by teachers: the roles of designer, implementer, and evaluator.

BUDDY SYSTEM (ACCOUNTABILITY PARTNERS)

In light of the larger responsibility put on learner's shoulders, I have noticed that the buddy system, finding a partner to share in your accomplishments and hold you accountable to your daily, weekly, and monthly tasks, is very effective.

A buddy, or if you prefer a more formal title, "accountability partner," provides a source to share information, ask questions, and commiserate with. It is my view that a shared online experience is perhaps one of the most powerful ways to curb the dropout rate and increase your chances to complete a given objective.

I report my daily efforts to my accountability partners, letting them know what I am reading, watching, and doing. In turn, my accountability partner shares valuable resources with me, and gives feedback that I need.

THE FEYNMAN TECHNIQUE

One last technique that may prove useful to you as you develop your ecosystem is the Feynman technique. The Feynman technique is a mental model that teachers use to help better explain difficult concepts to students; in other words, the technique suggests that to know something, you must be able to explain it.

Feynman believed that if you cannot explain it, you don't know it well enough. He explains, "The first principle is that you must not fool yourself, and you are the easiest person to fool."

What is great about this technique for self-directed learning is that it gives you the chance to assume the role of teacher...to yourself. In other words, this technique can help you become a better self-instructor, which is key when organizing a self-directed learning system. Here are four steps:

1. DECIDE ON A TOPIC. Feynman suggests first writing down what you already know on the topic and then commit yourself to study, adding to your notes things that you previously did not know or understand so that you have a list of items.

2. EXPLAIN THE TOPIC. After you gather a sizable amount of information, it is time for you to test your ability to explain it. You can pretend you are in front of a classroom or simply speak aloud to yourself (this is yet another example of the think aloud technique we previously shared). Think of examples and/or organizational devices (like a numbered list) to make it easy to understand.

3. REALIZE WHERE YOU FALL SHORT. After your performance, think about where you got stuck, what you didn't know, and go back to your study. Pay attention to the gaps in your knowledge and make those the areas of focus.

4. SIMPLIFY YOUR KNOWLEDGE. The last step is to distill the information you have learned into a sharp series of facts, making sure that your imaginary classroom could understand the information you present. You may want to identify analogies that connect the facts to the real world to simplify things further.

ONE MORE THING

My 15-year-old daughter is learning to drive. Scary, I know. One thing that has been interesting to note is that my daughter, who has traveled the same roads with my wife and I for as long as she can remember, has changed her view of these roads now that she is in the driver's seat. While she has been a passenger for years, by taking the wheel in her hands, there is naturally a greater burden of responsibility. She often comments about "finally understanding where things are," meaning that while she had witnessed us take her to school, church, and friends' homes, now that she herself has become the driver, she is making all kinds of connections she otherwise would not have.

To connect that small story to online language learning, I imagine that many of you have had teachers that have told you what to learn and how to learn it. In some sense, they have always been in charge of the steering wheel, and there is great comfort in that. However, with the movement toward online learning, and with the concept of an ecosystem in mind, I hope you are excited for the greater learning gains that are yours for the taking just by sitting in the driver's seat.

In our final chapter of this section, let's explore four more ways to do just that.

Because you are in charge of your own curriculum, you must change the way you learn.

DETAILS OF SELF-DIRECTED LEARNING

Being your own language teacher is not a slapdash, disorganized task. As illustrated in the last chapter, it requires understanding a bit more about the teaching craft, about motivational drivers, and about how to select between alternate modes of learning. It also requires the ability to recognize the difference between good and bad online resources, and how to mix those resources to optimize results. Above all, it demonstrates a need for learners to learn *how* they learn.

When I first encountered Barbara Oakley's material, I knew she was on to something. It began like this. I had been contemplating my first foray into online educational design, and my department was approached by Coursera, the largest massive open online course platform, who gave us the green light to create courses of our own choosing.

I couldn't believe my luck. I had been considering an online teacher-training program for years and had kept hundreds of pages of notes since my days in Iraq. As a teacher trainer in my heart of hearts, I wanted to give a gift to the English teacher community that would be a lasting one. I conceived of a

TESOL Certificate program, the standard in my field, but one that would be entirely online. On top of that, it would be world class.

As I conceived of this design, I was given a crash course on Coursera's platform, which was unique in several regards. While it was similar to most online platforms in basic features (video lectures, online quizzes, and discussion boards), it had added features that I enjoyed such as instant polling, reminders, and progress-tracking features that were good for self-directed learning. It also allowed learners to post videos in a way that I realized promoted not only valuable feedback but could create a sense of community and friendship. The more I explored, the more I was certain that I could create an entire industry standard certificate using these tools.

I was also given several courses that might serve as models, and one in particular caught my eye. It was a course called Learning How to Learn from Dr. Barbara Oakley.

The course design was simple but clear, and Oakley's approach was warm and inviting, sharing metaphors and strong visuals that supported those metaphors. Using principles of neuroscience to ground her content, she explained that learning how to learn was an oft-neglected topic, but that once addressed, could give learners powerful tools to master "any subject."

I watched the videos and immediately recognized the strength of what she was doing. Not only was the content good, but she modeled her very own principles in her course design. I knew I had found a likeminded designer, and I was impressed with her careful attention to detail and her main message. By teaching people to learn how to learn, it allows people to sit in the driver's seat.

Here are three Barbara Oakley-inspired techniques that will help you improve your focus and increase your productivity.

POMODORO

A Pomodoro is a technique that eliminates distraction and allows you to hyper focuson a topic. The Pomodoro technique was popularized by Francesco Cirillo in the late 1980s and consisted of using a timer to break down work, most traditionally into 25-minute intervals. (*Pomodoro* means *tomato*, which was said to be the shape of the timer Cirillo had as a university student.)

Put simply, the idea of a Pomodoro is to set aside all tasks, put on a timer, and then, for 25 minutes, work feverishly on that task alone.This means that, during the 25 minutes spent, a person using the Pomodoro technique should not use cellphones, email, social media, conversation, food, or any other distractions from interfering with the task at hand (this may mean either working in a place that allows that kind of privacy, or creating a place inside your head that allows you to focus amidst distraction).

SELECTIVE ATTENTION

Selective attention comes from a theory that, at times, educators must point out certain features of language to students in order to help those students acquire them. Educators, in this sense, invited students to notice certain grammatical forms in otherwise authentic material.

This led to the idea that you could expose learners to a number of these forms in order for them to first notice the form, then learn about the form, and then finally, acquire the form. The concept of an "input flood" was developed to demonstrate that a teacher might choose or create material that had a large number of these forms. For example, an educator might choose the song *Hoping and Wishing* in order to demonstrate the different uses of gerunds in English.

A number of theorists have discussed the importance of having students notice a feature in order for them to acquire it. It appears almost entirely impossible for learners to pick up on certain features unless they are exposed and made aware of them. Richard Schmidt (1990) argues that an important part of language acquisition is noticing something consciously, and while that is in contrast with Stephen Krashen's view that learning something simply *isn't* the same as acquiring it, Lightbown (1985) suggests that perhaps formal instruction can create "hooks, points of access" because learners can notice something new that they didn't before.

To use this technique as self-directed language learners, once again, you will have to be your own instructor. This means that you will have to carefully look for forms that you are just beginning to notice. If you are unaware of certain features in language, you may want to spend time taking tests or quizzes and see where you may need additional focus on form.

Selective attention should also mean that, while you may make errors in other areas, your focus is turned away from those errors (at least for a time) as you work on improving in just a single skill area. Thus, for example, you may look only at verb conjugation one week and then spend time on phrasal verbs the next week. In other words, you selectively pay attention to certain forms of your own choice, and then pay attention to other forms later on.

DEEP PRACTICE/CHUNKING

Deep practice is a technique wherein you focus in on the details of something in order to master it. It might be a small musical phrase for a musician, or a single move in basketball. In language, deep practice refers to identifying a form and seeking to master that form. The form might be grammatical, lexical, or auditory. A learner often identifies an error or difficulty and then works on it through a series of steps.

Step 1: UNDERSTAND THE WHOLE THING. The first step is to try to understand the whole of the skill you are hoping to master.

Step 2: BREAK IT INTO PIECES OR "CHUNKS." This is often the work that teachers do to help students understand something. A teacher, when giving you something beyond your level of ability, often tries to break down the different components of something so that you can better understand it. For example, if you were learning music with three difficult rhythms, the teacher might take each of these three rhythms and work on them separately. The idea behind separating out difficult bits of information is that, in isolation, you can target them with more frequency and focus. You are then more likely to perform the action fluidly and automatically.

Step 3: SLOW DOWN AND DO IT AGAIN. After identifying the different steps or chunks, the next step is to slow down each chunk, one by one, and then, gradually, as you master each chunk, you can repeat it at a faster rate.

Step 4: MAKE IT NATURAL. Finally, you can go back to absorbing the entire whole of the skill again. Return to it and see how the chunks fit together. Often, this involves visualization. For learners of language, "make it natural" also means that when you see or hear something that is not correct, it "feels" incorrect. Some might suggest, in fact, that it should bother you, like a musician who hears a wrong note or a baker that tastes something wrong in a recipe. When you can hear correct and incorrect language forms, an action often referred to as "noticing," you will have gained a valuable skill to help you monitor your own learning progress. (For a fuller description of chunking, Daniel Coyle's *The Talent Code* is particularly good.)

FINAL THOUGHTS

I am convinced that self-directed learning, and learning how to learn, is a key to educating future generations. Students, both young and old, now have more access to information than ever in the history of the world and will need more and more tools in order to learn not only how to access it, but how to learn it. Paying attention to detail in language learning, like my Japanese executives, will give you a clear advantage over other language learners, and can help to make your online learning a success.

As a side note, I wanted to thank Dr. Barbara Oakley one more time. Her course design and the principles found within them gave me the inspiration for my own course designs.

Just a short two years after I watched Barb present her course (which, to date, is the largest online course ever produced in the world), my colleagues and I received Coursera's Learner First Award. Out of more than 1,600 courses, ours stood out as the best in completion ratings and student reviews. It is currently the largest TESOL Certificate program in the world, and has exceeded my wildest dreams.

Learning a language through the ecosystem model requires you to get lost in the flow of work (using Pomodoros, selective attention and deep practice).

27.5 NOT EVEN A CHAPTER, JUST A THOUGHT

As a teacher, I have learned to spot you. I will pass out a work-sheet in a classroom, and almost all the students groan, but not you. Or if you do groan, it is only in response to everyone else around you. After all, you don't want classmates to know your dirty little secret.

You love worksheets. You love the idea of knocking things out one by one. You love taking on a task, one that is solvable, bite-sized, and developed by someone else. You probably like puzzles too, you weirdo.

For those of you who love worksheets, I wanted to remind you that the last section of the book presents to you a series of worksheets that will help you practice the techniques discussed throughout. These worksheets were especially developed for those of you that need just a little more guidance, a little more detail, to understand the techniques and how to put them into practice.

And then there are the rest of you. Those of you who hate worksheets. I can hear the phrase "busy work" make its way from your brain toward your lips.

Let me just remind you again the need for you, at least occasionally, to put on your nerd glasses and take out your pocket protector and then focus on some of the difficult aspects of language learning: the detailed, focused aspects.

By setting aside time each week, you'll find your language learning skyrocket, your social prospects improve, and everyone will find your command of language makes you appear smarter, more sophisticated, and more attractive. And what is cooler than that?

Small weekly deposits will make your language bank grow.

PART VI
MEANING IS EVERYTHING

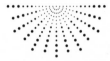

Words mean more than what is set down on paper. It takes the human voice to infuse them with shades of deeper meaning.

— MAYA ANGELOU

28

THREE YOUNG WOMEN

THREE YOUNG WOMEN WALKED INTO MY CLASSROOM. THEY were all from the same country, but that detail distracts from the point, since dozens of countries might have produced these same three. These three came in with a belief system that learning a language meant nothing more than passing a language test, and success on the test was what mattered most.

During a spring semester, these three young women walked into my college preparation classroom and I noticed them immediately. They were a wall of frowns, a unified front and a testament to cohesiveness that for some strange reason reminded me of a cross-cultural game of Red Rover. They stared straight ahead, shoulders evenly spaced, in a manner reminiscent of an unusually dour group of synchronized swimmers.

I began teaching in my usual style, all smiles and involvement. I shared how important it is that we become a family, and I shared how it was my goal to teach them that college was like a separate nation, with its own customs and traditions. I told them I would be their tour guide as we explored the boundaries of this new, undiscovered country. I was in fine teaching form, getting students to participate, asking them to elaborate on their own fears and understanding of language, and attempting to open them up to a new world.

Even still, the three students approached me shortly after class, single file.

"We don't need," spoke the shortest. "We only need TOEFL." The others nodded in assent. They were referring to the college entrance test given to non-native English speakers. This was a typical complaint: that my class was not preparing students for their most immediate need.

"Oh?" I said. "Well, I'll be teaching you a lot of TOEFL techniques that will definitely help you."

They did not budge. "Only TOEFL."

For the next few weeks, I insisted that my class would indeed help them for the test and beyond, but these three young students (whom I grew to admire, by the way), would sit in the back, arms often crossed, and refuse to participate.

A short time later, they began bringing TOEFL books to class, and they would quietly study. Some time after that, they sat outside my classroom and studied their books during my class time. I did my best to involve them, but they were adamant. The test was what mattered. All other considerations were secondary. Their logic was simple and overpowering.

That is not to say they were mean-spirited. They even invited me over to their apartment once. Up the steps and past dozens of American apartments, I walked into a door and was struck by the smells and sounds of a foreign country. In fact, it was as if the door were a portal, and I had been whisked away to a far-off land. I asked them if they were going to the American party I had noticed downstairs. I asked them if they had met any American friends. *No, only TOEFL* was again the reply. I believe they shared this as an attempt to brag about their focus. I nodded.

I learned that they had each studied anywhere from 10 to 12 hours daily, pouring themselves into their books like ascetics would the Dead Sea Scrolls. They had put in the work. I was so impressed with them. I still am.

About a month later, they came to me with triumph in their eyes. They were holding sheets of paper: their TOEFL scores. They announced to me that they had understood all along what path would lead them to victory.

"Teacher," said one, "we were right. And you were wrong." Such directness from certain cultures used to offend me, but it does not anymore. Anyway, in their celebratory mood, I did not argue the point. It is difficult to argue with smiles. I congratulated them and told them good luck. They all left for the university shortly thereafter.

What happened after is something I will always remember. One of the students described it like this:

I went to the university class the first day. The teacher began talking like you, really, with all the Americans talking back. I could not understand the teacher and I could not understand anything. When I did understand, I could not share my understanding. The teacher assigned a five-page paper. A five-page paper of my own thoughts and ideas? How could I? What could I do? I went home and I cried. This place is not for me. It is a place I do not know.

My heart broke for them as each told me much the same story. They had attained a level of linguistic competence that was well suited for tests, but not suited for actual conversation and real life language use. All three of them dropped out of the university within weeks. They arrived on the doorsteps of my tiny school, once again, a short time later.

Three girls came to my office, heads slightly bowed. Several of them began speaking at once, telling me their stories.

"Teacher," one smiled wryly, perhaps recognizing the symmetry of her remark, and said, "we were wrong, and you were right."

29

LEARN A LITTLE, USE IT A LOT

THE STORY OF THE THREE YOUNG WOMEN DEMONSTRATES HOW a number of language learners approach the task of learning. They memorize, study in order to achieve rote knowledge, and in so doing, fail to recognize the importance of applying that knowledge to real contexts. Unsurprisingly, learners who take this approach to language (let's call it 'memorize, test, forget, repeat') usually find it harmful to their progress.

This concept has been discussed by researchers in a number of different ways, but perhaps one of the most useful comes from the distinction that theorists make between learning about a language and learning a language. Learning *about* a language refers to memorizing vocabulary, studying grammatical principles, and amassing as many 'units' of language as possible. In this view of language learning, the more you collect, the more you know.

To illustrate, it is quite common for students of Latin to learn in just this fashion. Latin, you see, is a dead language, meaning no one actually speaks it today in the modern world. When it is taught, students are rarely invited to have a conversation in it.

Primarily, learners study the 'memorize, test, forget, repeat' method, or what Francois Gouin referred to earlier as the "classical" method.

In fact, let's imagine that you are a Latin student right now in a typical class, and somehow you get magically whisked away to ancient Rome. "How?" you ask. I don't know; humor me. If you need further detail, let's just say you fell into a wormhole next to your desk while you were picking up a pencil. Better? Okay.

Now let's imagine further that you are captured by a Latin-speaking emperor, and noticing your strange clothes, he demands you explain who you are and how you have come into the city. You are told that if you explain yourself reasonably, you will be given a seat next to him, and a chance to marry his beautiful daughter or handsome son. However, if you can't explain yourself, you will have to choose between a good old-fashioned burning or a hanging in the royal courtyard. Once again, he tells you to speak immediately or face death.

So, in the end, faced with either imminent death or the chance to sit on a royal throne, what do you think of your prospects? Well, I hate to be the bearer of bad news, but I'd say you aren't likely to be hearing wedding bells.

You see, while motivation would likely not be a problem for you in these dire circumstances, I'm afraid your motivation would do little to help you. You would likely notice that your ability to communicate is nonexistent, and that there is a large gap between how much you know and how much you can say. As you open your mouth to explain yourself, you find that your knowledge about inflected nouns, declensions, and the ablative and dative cases in Latin are of little help. In fact, it is quite likely that even the vocabulary and grammar that you learned on the very last test has mostly been forgotten.

The story of opening your mouth and finding that nothing comes to mind is rather common (but at least not the part where you likely die a horrible death). The fact remains that the story among learners is so common that scientists are constantly trying to understand why certain kinds of learning don't transfer to applicable skills. Neuroscientists have recently had a lot to say about this concept, and are beginning to help language learning experts piece together how the brain actually acquires a language. These neuroscientists are demonstrating precisely why the memorize, test, forget, repeat method is unsuitable to a language learning program.

To understand the neuroscience behind language learning, let's talk about Legos. Legos, as you most likely know already, are interlinking toys that people use to build cars, buildings, planes, or whatever a child wants. The purpose of Legos is to build something—anything—that you want. There are endless combinations, and although there are thousands of different kinds of Legos, most people quickly realize that with a typical box of the most common Legos, it is surprising how inventive one can be. You can create (with just a few Legos) quite a lot.

In a similar way, good language learners realize that vocabulary and grammar are not just items you collect; rather, the purpose behind them is to build, although in this case, you are building sentences or entire conversations. Even with just one "box" full of vocabulary and grammar, the inventive learner can come up with countless combinations that allow quite a number of acceptable conversations.

The brain, you see, doesn't easily store and remember individual units of information. It prefers to store by connecting bits of information to each other through the creation of neural networks. By connecting certain pieces together (again, think of Legos), your brain starts to discover and use common patterns, often referred to as chunks.

These chunks give you more brain space, which opens up opportunities for you to make your conversations increasingly complex. By connecting bits of information together, you, in essence, form patterns that some neuroscientists refer to as *neural highways* that metaphorically helps us understand how information, through these large networks can zip across quickly and efficiently.

In other words, and I can't stress this enough, memory comes in the *connecting* of bits of information more than the *collecting*. Thus, your primary job when it comes to language learning is not to amass units of information, rather it is to use those bits of information in multiple combinations as soon and often as possible. While we could get into the neuroscience even further, for now let's just distill this idea into a simple phrase: *Learn a little, use it a lot*.

The "learn a little" concept suggests that rather than studying all the possible vocabulary and grammar for any possible situation you run into, a better approach is to learn just some vocabulary and grammar, and then manage (or in the Lego metaphor, play with) only that amount. Some theorists refer to this working system as a metalanguage. It isn't perfect, it isn't complete, but it is a start. By learning to command and control just a little bit of language, you are much more likely to store language in your active, working memory.

So, while there's nothing wrong with focusing on the details of language, without using, practicing, and building with the bits of language you are gathering, you will quickly discover that when asked to speak, nothing comes out, and this is true because you simply haven't created the neural connections that would allow success. You are not a poor learner; you just haven't understood how your brain works.

Learning just a few words, phrases, and grammatical structures, especially the most common building blocks, you'll do a lot better. In the next chapter, we'll discuss what those common building blocks might look like.

For now, just remember to live by the phrase *Learn a little, use it a lot*. By so doing, if you ever do get sucked down a wormhole while studying Latin and find yourself staring at an emperor asking you which path to choose, you'll have the ability to say *I choose to live* in Latin: *Ego nolo vivere.*

May I also suggest you add *Tollet de pulcherrimus alter a sinistra.* I'll take the good-looking one on the left.

Learn a little, use it a lot.

BUILDING BLOCKS

As soon as I start talking about modern corpus linguistics, I start to lose people. In fact, this even happens at conferences where people have a major interest in language learning. If I risk sharing data or throwing out a phrase like "the number of lexemes in modern corpora," I will immediately get people yawning, staring at their watches, or checking their phones.

Conversely, rather than losing people by spitting out the data, if I start talking about what the data means, people begin to perk up, start taking notes, and nod approvingly. You see, while this brand of linguistics may sound dull at the onset, the implications of current corpus linguistics research can get people on the edge of their seats. To put it another way, no one really cares about the science behind the flux capacitor, just so long as it makes time travel possible.

In corpus linguistics, scientists peer into language by analyzing a large group of texts, often with millions of words. Again, there are certainly boring aspects to this job. Some of these scientists, for example, have individually tagged each word into its respective part of speech, just like a marine biologist would tag sea creatures in the ocean. *Is this a noun, verb, adjective, mollusk, or clam?*

They have also identified clauses, tenses, prepositional phrases, and other bits of linguistic information. With millions of words in these large *corpora* (plural of *corpus*), you can imagine how tedious the work might get. Thank you, corpus linguists, for doing the dirty work no one else wants to do. Mike Rowe would be proud.

With this kind of investigative study, researchers are able to determine word and grammatical frequency. Therefore, a linguist might find out the answers to these kinds of questions:

- How common is the word *xiào* in Chinese?
- How common is the subjunctive mood in Spanish?
- How is the honorific *sama* in Japanese used—and is it more common in writing or in speaking?

Linguists can now ask thousands of questions in front of their computers, and computers will generate an answer instantaneously.

So, over the course of 30 plus years, what have corpus linguists and educators learned? Well, some of the things we have learned are rather predictable. For example, the most common pronoun used in spoken languages, is the word *I* (we humans love to talk about ourselves). Articles such as *the* and *a* usually make it in a top ten list of languages where articles are present. The most common verb in many languages? The *be* verb, of course.

You can quickly scan the internet for top 100 lists in many languages, and you can even see how, historically, words have changed in meaning and fallen in and out of popular use.

You might be tempted to say, then, that during all the time

that corpus linguists have been peering under the hood of each language car, we have arrived at a number of rather interesting but inconsequential observations and perhaps a few items of passing interest. I think that is a fair assessment when looking at any of these given answers out of a broader context.

However, there is another way of looking at the data of corpus linguistics. Rather than looking narrowly by examining individual questions based on word frequency, meaning, and usage, when linguists take a more bird's eye view by examining similarities between languages, then some fascinating patterns emerge. Let me discuss two of these larger patterns.

First, among these patterns between often-dissimilar languages is a remarkable number. The number is 2,000. Linguists have discovered that 2,000 words accounts for a whopping 80% coverage in most corpora.

What does this mean? It means that if someone were to learn the most common 2,000 words of the sometimes million or more in any given language, they would likely recognize about 80% of the words spoken or written in almost any given corpus. Spanish, German, English, you name it, 2,000 of the most common words is sort of a magic barometer if you will, for what might be called a foundational entry into a language (O'Keefe, McCarthy, and Carter, 2007; Davies, 2002; Jones, 2003).

It does not stop there, however. With the next 2,000 words, (so now you have 4,000 words), often you can get to 90% coverage, and with another 2,000 more, you can get to well over 95%. While perhaps not as large an overall percentage as your first 2,000 words, with 6,000 words and 95% plus coverage, it is likely that you, armed with these foundational words, would understand a great majority of anything thrown at you.

A similar pattern also exists when examining grammatical items such as tense, and I will stick to an English example for this one, since there is greater variability among languages when it comes to tense (Chinese, for example, does not even have verb conjugations, so tense isn't really what we discuss when learning to specify time or aspect in Chinese).

Keith Folse, a renowned language instructor and lover of corpus linguistics, once invited a group of educators to guess, without the use of corpus data, the most common tense in the English language. I will invite you to do the same here.

What is the most common tense in English, written or spoken?

Many of the teachers that day chose the past tense, thinking that when most people speak, they are often referring to completed actions in the past. Some teachers chose the present progressive (*I am walking, we are talking*, etc.), since all of us live our lives in the immediate present.

However, you may be surprised to learn that the simple present tense (*I am/she is/we are*) is easily the winner. In fact, the simple present tense represents about 60% of all the verbs found in most corpora. If you add the simple past and simple future, you can account for just over 85%, and with just 5 of the 12 commonly taught tenses in English, 98% of all language is accounted for (Ginseng, 2017).

This may not sound earth shattering to you, but as Dr. Folse revealed much of this same data, a number of us hung our head in shame. Why? Because we tend to teach units in grammar books, and we teach the present tense in equal amounts (in fact, I find that because the 'present tense' is considered the easiest, it is often taught the least).

Corpus linguistics directly challenges this belief, or at the very least gives us pause, forcing us to think about whether the past perfect progressive tense is really a unit we should spend two weeks teaching, especially when it is used less than one tenth of one percent of the time in actual spoken or written English.

The collective gasp I heard from the crowd that day was not because corpus linguistics data is so interesting, but because it revealed that we as teachers were wasting much of our teaching lives by not paying attention to the data. The data, in short, tells us we are collecting Legos instead of playing with the most common building blocks.

So what does this mean to a self-directed language learner such as yourself? Again, let's go back to our earlier chapter theme, and say one more time, it is important to learn a little, and use it a lot.

In this case, with just a fraction of the words that a native speaker might have, you can get along pretty well, and you don't need to gather all of the 20,000 words that a native language speaker might have in order to do pretty well. The truth is that with just 2,000 words you will do all right, and with 6,000, you will do more than all right. With a vocabulary like that, you'd be able to speak at a language conference in Bogota, Colombia, just like I did last year.

QUICK TIP FOR MOST LANGUAGES

- To achieve a beginning level of a language, start with 2,000 and 2 tenses (present and past)
- To achieve an intermediate level of a language, learn 4,000 words and 4 tenses (present, past, future, and perfect)
- To achieve an advanced level of a language, learn 6,000 words and 6 tenses (present, past, future, perfect, progressive, and perfect progressive)

Note: if your language does not have the same kinds of verb conjugations listed above, you may want to investigate what common verb conjugations do exist. In the case of Chinese, for example, it is useful to learn constructions for present, past, future, and how to express something that happens repeatedly.

With just a few words and even fewer grammar structures, you can attain a beginning, intermediate, and advanced level of language.

THE CASE FOR FUN

IN THE LAST TWO CHAPTERS I ATTEMPTED TO EXPLAIN THE need for a *Learn a little, use it a lot* mentality. This frame of mind often increases motivation in students as they realize that it is not necessary to learn every single word in order to be a successful language learner. These chapters demonstrate that if you come armed with just a fraction of the words of a native speaker; you can be at least moderately successful navigating a book, a movie, or even a country.

This strategy strikes fear into the heart of the perfectionist, however, who more often than not does not want to make any mistakes. Speaking of perfectionist, while this chapter is for everyone, I want to pay particular attention to those of you who identify as perfectionists and provide you some additional tips. To begin with, for those of you who struggle because of a need to get things right all the time, let me begin by saying that you are likely to be better off if, at least in moments, you think of language learning as fun.

Many studies (and common sense) bear this out. Language learners traditionally have a balanced approach wherein they not only work hard, but they let loose and find things they truly enjoy (I identified this learner trait in the first section as an "active" approach).

My conversations with thousands of language learners confirm these studies, and I am always impressed by how passionately people share with me the kinds of "fun" resources that opened them up to language learning. It seems everyone has an opinion on the best shows, music, movies, and videos. People feel attached to them, as if they were sharing a private secret or a hidden pathway to learning that they alone discovered.

For my mother, it was *I Love Lucy*. *I Love Lucy* is a sitcom classic starring Lucille Ball and Desi Arnaz. My mother first came to the United States as a young wife, leaving her hometown of Durango, Mexico to follow my father in his university studies. While in the States, my mother became involved in the community by attending English classes and finding friends. While the classes and friendships helped, my mother is quick to point out that these were not the only resources she found useful, and, in fact, she attributes much of her language learning to this fictional television program.

When she began to watch the show, the first thing my mother discovered was how much she enjoyed it, from the way that Lucy got herself in and out of predicaments to the way she interacted with her husband and best friends (Ethel and Fred). My mother discovered that she could understand much of the physical comedy even when she did not understand the words. In addition, she related to Desi Arnaz's character Ricky, who was from Cuba and sometimes did not understand English as well as he would like. My mother started to lose herself in the show, and ignored the fact that it was in English at all. Soon, she was *focused entirely on meaning*.

Let us discuss this very crucial phrase, *focused on meaning*, since it is such a major point of emphasis in language learning circles and the title of this entire section of chapters.

While different theorists speak about "a focus on meaning" in slightly different ways, perhaps the easiest way to talk about it is to say that it is the opposite of a "focus on grammar" (or what others still call a "focus on form").

When a learner or teacher focuses on meaning, they look at the entire whole rather than the details (an entire book, a full conversation, or, in my mother's case, a complete show). When successful, a focus on meaning is a way of losing yourself in the material, of ignoring the things you do not know and, thus, enjoying what you are doing. By so doing, you maintain motivation and continue to encounter more language.

A number of researchers contend that this approach is much better than a focus on form, which constantly threatens to point out what you do not know.

Oh, yeah, and a focus on meaning is fun, and teachers revel in the fact that they can involve students in ways that get them to forget their fears. Truthfully, a focus on meaning has become more than a language learning approach; it is almost a philosophical viewpoint or way of life.

Now let me stop here and again reiterate that I am neither a "focus on form" nor a "focus on meaning" theorist. It is my view, and again, I think the studies bear this out, that the best learners know how to bounce from one style to the other, and perhaps more importantly, know WHEN to switch (we'll discuss that in the next chapter).

However, since I am addressing those who may struggle a bit with attempting the "focus on meaning" approach, I want to give two very specific tips so that you perfectionists can, to put it quite frankly, loosen up. (Seriously. Why are your shoulders so tense?)

FORTRESS OF SOLITUDE

The first tip is simple. One of the reasons that perfectionists struggle with a focus on meaning approach is because no matter how much you tell a perfectionist that it is good/fun/exciting to make mistakes, the perfectionist knows better. Mistakes are horrible, and making them in front of others even worse. If you ever find yourself in the perfectionist camp, you will be happy to know that much of the focus on meaning approach can be done in solitude with absolutely no one around.

To you I recommend a fortress of solitude. The Fortress of Solitude, for those of you who remember the movie *Superman*, was the place that our caped wonder built away from everyone. It was a retreat from human companionship; a place where he could learn all that he could. Upon leaving the Fortress of Solitude, he felt prepared to take on the world. In a similar way, a fortress of solitude for a language learner is a place for you to study alone, feel prepared, and then take on the world.

Just to be clear, however, I am not advocating that you collect language pieces like Francois Gouin or the three young women; rather, I recommend that you make your isolation time, your language learning, fun. Download movies, watch TV shows, write down imaginary conversations, and simply enjoy the language. You'll find that making your alone time fun and interesting will likely give you more fun and interesting topics to discuss when you feel prepared to leave your own personal fortress and engage the world of humans.

So please, please, please, make sure you have fun, even when you are studying on your own. In self-directed learning, if your curriculum is boring, out of touch with the learner, or otherwise inappropriate, you only have yourself to blame. So assign yourself something you enjoy.

PRACTICE SESSIONS

As you create your fortress of solitude, you might want to think of it as a time to perform practice sessions. Practice sessions, like the name implies, are times you set aside to focus on and practice language tasks, especially the kind you will perform in the future. The closer your preparation is to actual future performance, the better your performance is likely to be.

In fact, as you practice what you will perform, you'll notice that your confidence increases and your fear dissipates. Rather than thinking of confidence as an immutable personality trait, you'll learn the truth: you aren't born with confidence, you cultivate it.

Have fun (even when you are alone).

A TWO-TRACK MIND

WHILE THERE IS CONVINCING EVIDENCE THAT YOU SHOULD focus on both details and meaning, on bits of language and whole conversations, a key question arises: WHEN should you engage in a focus on form, and when should you engage in a focus on meaning? Neuroscience provides answers, especially as we learn how the brain learns in two very specific modes, the focused and diffuse mode.

The focused mode of learning is very much in line with the section we discussed about detail, or what we called a focus on form. A focused mode of learning is what we typically think of when we think of study: alone at a desk, cramming for a test, trying to memorize facts and ideas.

The diffuse mode, on the other hand, is quite the opposite. It is associated with a more relaxed style of thinking, one that allows the mind to wander and make connections between apparently unrelated ideas, much as you might do as you are going to bed at night or waking up in the morning. Many people find that they engage in the diffuse mode best when in the shower, or perhaps driving to work. If you have ever had an idea that you simply had to write down, something that came unexpectedly as you were lying in bed, this idea likely came from having been in the diffuse mode of thinking. The diffuse mode helps you make connections that otherwise would never have occurred to you, and is often associated with innovation and problem solving. Researchers are discovering that the diffuse mode of thinking operates especially during periods of relaxation, exercise, or even sleep.

To get back to our original question of when, now let us apply these two modes of thinking to language learning.

The diffuse mode, as our examples above hint at, is often the correct choice when you are faced with the need to create or to solve a problem. It allows innovation to occur, and thus, might be the mode you choose when you are stuck or frustrated with a new problem you cannot solve. Thus, it can be very useful in the writing process, or when drafting out a speech or conversation that you would like to perform. There is a sort of freeform or free association quality to the diffuse mode, meaning that by giving yourself time and space to think, you can often think of a great variety of ways to do a similar task.

However, the diffuse mode is also useful when it comes to listening and speaking, especially when engaging in the kind of "learning for fun" approach mentioned in the last chapter. When you need to relax and recognize overall meanings (like the plot line to a movie, or the gist of a conversation), then a diffuse mode of learning is likely to be more beneficial than a focus on each individual detail or word in a conversation.

Finally, when you are in a real-time, speaking moment, when you "go live," so to speak, it is also probably best to engage in the diffuse mode of thinking. Relax, do not stress every detail, and focus on general meanings in order to get the most out of the moment.

The focused mode, on the other hand, can be used in traditional scenarios where you wish to apply your study in a serious manner, memorizing details, and learning in ways that require your undivided attention. However, even as I say this, I hope you recognize that this may result in the 'memorize, test, forget, and repeat' style that is so unproductive. In this case, let me suggest what may already be obvious to you: follow up a focused mode of study with a diffuse mode activity. Here are some tips on how:

BREAK UP STUDY WITH A CHANGE OF PACE

After intense moments of study, you may want to find a way to back off the study by engaging in a seemingly meaningless activity, like talking with a friend or eating a small treat. You might want to read something for fun—something completely unrelated.

What often happens after moments of study is that the brain simply needs time to make connections stronger, and often, engaging in either a complete break or a more "diffuse" activity, you will find that your brain is refreshed. In fact, it may even be that the problems you are working on are clearer. This is because the diffuse mode of thinking can, metaphorically, work in the background while you perform non-focused tasks, thinking of solutions for you that will be useful when you return to a focused mode of learning.

BREAK UP STUDY WITH EXERCISE AND SLEEP

Another important aspect of your brain is that it tends to work very well during moments just before and after sleep. That is why I mentioned the idea of getting up out of bed to write down a good idea. When you are in a relaxed state, your brain is more likely to make connections it wouldn't otherwise make. Similarly, studies have also demonstrated that exercise has a way of boosting your endorphins and relaxing your body, which in turn, allows the diffuse mode to engage more fully.

All in all, I recommend the diffuse mode of learning, especially in tandem with the kind of "fun" focused-on-meaning approach I mention in the earlier chapters. I believe that by doing so, you'll find that you don't burn out from language study, and you'll actually feel refreshed physically as well as mentally. Beyond that, you'll find that the diffuse mode increases memory by helping solidify neural connections, and supports your more deliberate study.

The truth is, when it comes to how your brain actually works, you don't have a one-track mind at all. You, my clever friend, have a two-track mind, and the best way to maximize your results is to learn how, and when, to use both tracks.

The diffuse mode of learning allows you to make connections and see overall patterns. Exercise, sleep, and a change of pace improve your ability to engage in this mode.

33.5 NOT EVEN A CHAPTER, JUST SOME ADVICE

A language learner ecosystem is a powerful weapon for anyone wanting to conquer a language. That stated, where does this put teachers? Are they no longer relevant? How about the classroom itself? How is language learning shifting, and what can language teachers do to accommodate that shift?

While the majority of those who read this book are not or will not be language teachers, I wanted to share just one word of advice to those who are. If you are a language teacher and find yourself trying to understand how the ecosystem model might be implemented for your own learners, let me suggest that you see yourself in two pivotal ways.

First of all, continue to be a language builder. Help students lay a foundation for understanding language by helping them to recognize the sounds, vocabulary (2,000-6,000 words), grammatical units (4-6 tenses), and other aspects of language that they will need to engage with the outside world.

Second, make sure you see yourself as a spark. Your job is not only to provide language learners a foundation but to invite them to connect themselves to the real world. By inviting learners to see a world out there—one of friends, goals, books, and online resources, you are inviting them to see a world filled with possibility. In this sense, you can ignite a lifelong pursuit, one that will carry far beyond the walls of the classroom.

If you are a language teacher, your role is now shifting. Your job is not only to build up students in the classroom but to ignite their interest to find resources outside it.

EPILOGUE

WHEN THE LEARNER IS READY, THE MASTER APPEARS

Let me close this book with some final thoughts. First and foremost, remember that the language learning ecosystem is not, and can never be, a formalized style or argument for how language must be done. It is a concept that should always retain flexibility, adapting to your own needs and purposes. In other words, while I have given strong recommendations on how you might approach language learning, especially through the prism of language learning strategies and neuroscience, ultimately, your ecosystem is your own, and you are the master of your own curriculum.

Secondly, let me remind you again about the importance of breaking a few eggs. Since we are dealing with a flexible system or approach, you should feel the freedom to experiment, and as you experiment, you should be willing to adjust as needed.

Speaking of experimentation, in order to accommodate your study, I have provided a series of worksheets that you may wish to use in order to expand on your learning. These worksheets should be used in any order and at any time, and should give you practical ideas for how to extend your language learner ecosystem.

As you continue to prepare yourself for language learning, may I remind you that as the master of your own language-learning destiny, you will find that your willingness to stay open is a key to your success. As the old saying goes, when the learner is ready, the master appears. In this case, the learner and the master…is you.

And you are ready.

PART VII
STRATEGY WORKBOOK

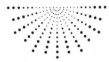

For each of the six major parts of this book, we have identified key strategies for you to work on building your language ecosystem.

The appendix that follows provides worksheets and information for you as you learn and practice language learner strategies. This section will expand or repeat the strategies introduced earlier in the book, and will give you practical worksheets to help you approach them.

These worksheets are organized according to the themes of these corresponding parts:

- Exploration (Part II)
- Introspection (Part III)
- Flexibility (Part IV)
- Focus on Details (Part V)
- Focus on Meaning (Part VI)

EXPLORE STRATEGY 1

GATHERING AND UTILIZING RESOURCES

A language ecosystem describes a holistic environment that encourages and extends the learning and application of languages beyond a classroom through a diverse system of activities and incentives (Dixon, 2017).

DEFINITION

One exciting new concept among educators might be referred to as the language learner ecosystem. The ecosystem concept suggests that language is learned not just in a classroom setting, but rather through a careful and deliberate creation of an environment conducive to language learning. In this sense, language can and should be everywhere around you, but must be discovered, cultivated, and engaged in order to work for you. When we refer to gathering and utilizing resources, we aren't just implying that you should "find some books," rather, we are asking you to consider putting yourself at the center of a language learner universe.

STUDY ON THE POWER OF GATHERING RESOURCES

Carol Griffiths' (2003) investigation into language learning strategies revealed that higher level language learners have a more sophisticated, interactive way of learning languages, including the "utilization of available resources." These savvy learners would not only identify and gather resources, but would use those resources to their great advantage. Griffiths mentions that the best learners in her study understood that language "involv[es] more manipulation...than memorization." A simple way to say this is that good language learners surround themselves in the target language, and then use their surroundings to practice.

STORY ON THE POWER OF GATHERING RESOURCES

In one particular case study (Naiman et al., 1978), an American referred to as "Ms. A" traveled to France, "with the expectation and intention of never returning to North America."

Even though her first few weeks were painful due to culture shock and a complete lack of French, Ms. A immediately went to work finding resources. She watched two French movies a day (American movies dubbed into French that she had already seen). She read in French: newspapers, magazines, and American comic books. She consulted a dictionary. She would listen in on conversations, and in perhaps the most extreme example of finding a useful resource, she married a Frenchman who loved learning languages (41-43). As a side note, we highly recommend falling in love as a source of language learning motivation!

THINK FIRST

Think about it yourself. Before reading some of our ideas, think about ways you could gather resources. What resources could you gather?

TRY IT OUT

1. FIND ENTERTAINMENT: Movies, books, and music can be excellent places to find authentic resources. For intermediate learners, streaming movies and shows are now common sources. Online websites dedicated to song lyrics can help you learn what your favorite bands are saying.

2. SEARCH OUT ONLINE APPS: There are a number of language learning apps and websites that are available, and many of them are free. A quick search in any search engine should reveal 100s of possible resources for 100s of languages.

3. GET BOOKS: Don't forget that the library can be your friend. While online resources can be a lot of fun, cozying up to a book can provide a very different experience that can help you experience exposure to language in a different way. For beginning learners, a beginning level textbook on your language can be extremely important.

4. TRAVEL: Of course, living in a place where the target language is spoken can be extremely useful. Planning trips or stays in a foreign country is about as immersive as you can get.

5. PEOPLE: One of the most important resources you have are the people that surround you. We will discuss finding people and joining a group in our second strategy.

A CAUTION ABOUT GATHERING RESOURCES

As Greg Scott, an online language learner, rightly warns, we must "stop hoarding language learning resources and start studying."

While gathering resources can be a fun task, like squirrels gathering nuts, Scott explains that hoarding is a form of procrastination. His tip is to keep it simple by having just one resource at a time.

Speaking of resources, for more free tips from Greg and other expert language learners, check out

https://www.lingualift.com/blog.

TRY IT OUT

Now think of different kinds of resources you don't have yet. Perhaps start with the sentence *What I'd love to get is...*

Personal Goal for Gathering Resources

EXPLORE STRATEGY 2

JOIN A LANGUAGE LEARNING NETWORK

DEFINITION

Language is social and demands interaction, thus, you must constantly find groups so you can practice. We call these groups, "language learning networks." Language learning networks might be found at work, at school, in a community, online, among neighbors, friends, or family. Gaining access to these networks (and in a different language) is not always easy: you may find that you don't have the same language level as other members, or that you don't share precisely the same interests.

Overcoming these differences often requires time and energy. Therefore, what often sets apart good language learners in groups is that they make themselves useful or interesting. In other words, to be a member of a group, you must primarily think about what you contribute to that group.

STUDY AND STORY ON THE POWER OF CREATING A LANGUAGE LEARNING NETWORK

In a study by Norton and Toohey (2001) researchers found a group of learners that all followed the good language learner strategies identified more than a decade earlier. However, one learner in particular, Eva, seemed to outshine the rest. How come? The researchers' conclusion was that she was able to negotiate entry into the social networks in her workplace.

Eva worked at a restaurant cleaning floors, and as an Italian immigrant in an English-speaking country, she had limited access to social networks where she might otherwise get involved. In fact, her position as a janitor made her feel "stupid" and her lack of English skills made her feel worthy of only "the worst kind of job " (315).

Regardless of her job status, Eva found creative ways to interact. First, while she initially couldn't find ways to interact at work and practice her English, monthly employee outings offered her the chance to accompany people (in her husband's car) to the outings and have employees meet her in an informal setting. This gave her the chance to talk, share ideas, and let them see her winning personality. Eventually, she was able to reposition herself from "immigrant" to a cultural and multilingual resource.

How'd she do it? For starters, she shared her vast knowledge of Europe with people, and even ended up helping people plan vacations there. She also shared her knowledge of Italian by giving one co-worker basic instruction in Italian phrases. Eva's ability to make her knowledge matter made people see her through new eyes. As her manager remarked, "you look really different when you are not at work." In short, Eva was able to find ways to get involved and most importantly, become *useful*.

TRY IT OUT

There are multiple ways to get involved in a group. One of the first things, of course, is to discover what groups exist.

1. DISCOVER PEOPLE: A friend or neighbor who speaks the target language can be a wonderful resource. You might consider having daily or weekly chats, or use these resources to ask questions you can't readily get from books or online.

2. DISCOVER COMMUNITY LEARNERS LIKE YOU: There may be community classes or even university classes near you. You might also look into clubs that share your language interest.

3. SHARE YOUR SKILLS: No matter what group you might join, you will want to think about skills or ideas that you can contribute. One of the easiest contributions you might have is your native language. If you are looking for a native speaker in Chinese, for example, you might want to find a Chinese speaker or group that is looking to improve their English.

4. ENTER A CHATROOM OR BLOG: You might want to enter a chatroom or visit a personal blog as well. Here you may find people who have similar interests as you. In a chatroom, you can practice your language skills by typing or speaking. By looking at blogs, you can respond in comment sections and enjoy what others are saying.

5. PERUSE SOCIAL MEDIA: Want to learn Swahili? There are interest pages for just about any language, and you can join groups that share your same love for learning, or, share a similar interest. Maybe you have a strong interest in Japanese kenpo, flower arranging,

temple rituals, or anime, for example—you'd be amazed what groups exist out there!

A CAUTION ABOUT JOINING A GROUP

You might want to think of joining a group a little bit like dating. Not every group will be a good fit for you. Some might speak too fast, some might have interests that are different from you, and some might not make it easy for you to contribute.

However, just like dating, sometimes persistence pays off. Don't just write off a group because they aren't easy to get to know. Remember that becoming a member of a group takes time and effort. Awkwardness is a stage we all go through when becoming a member of a new group.

SET A PERSONAL GOAL

Find a group that speaks the target language and join it. See what you can do to contribute to a group. You may need to plan out what you might say and do with that group. You might start with the sentence *A group I'd like to join is…*

Personal Goal for Joining a Group

EXPLORE STRATEGY 3

PREDICTION

DEFINITION

Prediction is a key strategy for language learning. It is, in its purest form, the act of guessing words, phrases, and grammatical patterns from context. It is what children do when they acquire their first language: listen, search for patterns and meaning, and apply what they hear to future conversations.

In fact, children most often learn new words or grammatical items by analogy (guessing in context) rather than by direct study. This is why children say *brang* instead of *brought*, or *thunk* instead of *thought*. They're paying attention to words such as *sing/ring* to guess the past of *bring*, and *sink/drink* to guess the past of *think*. In truth, they're simply making intelligent guesses by using the words they know and comparing them to words they aren't sure about. While they may make mistakes at times, their willingness to predict gives them an advantage.

STUDY ON PREDICTION'S POWER

So children do this, but can *you* learn through prediction? You bet. In one fascinating study (Saragi, Nation et al. 1978), adult learners were given a book, *A Clockwork Orange*, with over 241 nonsense words. In order to test if learners could learn from prediction (guessing in context) alone, the glossary of terms was not given to students. Even though they did not directly study any vocabulary lists, results demonstrated that, on average, learners— just by reading the book, remember—acquired 183 new words. That is the power of prediction.

STORY ON PREDICTION

As a young missionary in Venezuela, one language learner was constantly confronted with words he did not know. While in mid-conversation, he found it difficult to stop people every time and ask them what each individual word meant. One word, in partic-ular, made no sense to him. It sounded like *poet* or *po EH* to him. It was said at the beginning and ends of sentences, and some-times in the middle. After a time, he was too embarrassed to ask what the word meant because he heard it so often, but gradually began to understand that it was some sort of filler word like *then* or *you know*.

It was months later before he discovered that the word he was hearing time and time again was the word *pues*. This word, which can mean *well* or *so*, is extremely common in Venezuelan Span-ish, but the catch is that Venezuelans (and a number of Caribbean Spanish speakers) simply don't pronounce the *s*. Lucky thing he learned through listening and prediction; without knowing how to spell it, a dictionary couldn't have helped!

THINK FIRST

Before reading about some of our ideas on how to use prediction, think of ways that you have already used prediction in learning a language.

TRY IT OUT

There are many ways to improve or practice your ability to predict. Here are a few:

1. GUESS FROM A READING THAT IS A BIT TOO HARD. Take a reading that is a bit beyond your level (for every 20 words, 1 word is unfamiliar). Guess those words on a separate piece of paper. See how often you are correct.

2. GUESS FROM A MOVIE: Watch a movie in 5-minute segments without using subtitles. If needed, watch the movie several times until you feel comfortable that you can't learn anything more from it. Then go back and watch the movie with subtitles and see what you did and did not understand. Take a note of words or phrases that you correctly and/or incorrectly guessed.

3. PREDICT BEFORE YOU HEAR A THING: You can also predict even before you enter a conversation or engage in a reading. You can do this by examining the basic theme of the conversation. For example, if you are headed to a restaurant, you might write down all the words and phrases you think might be useful for a restaurant. You might also write down the words and phrases you DON'T know, and look them up. This will improve your ability to predict in the moment.

4. BE A NOTEBOOK HUNTER: Collect language chunks in a notebook as you engage in conversations. Language chunks are bits of language that often go together...phrases such as peanut butter and jelly, or see you later. Collecting chunks, phrases, idioms, and so forth will help you to master a language. As a side benefit, many people are much more patient with you when you demonstrate you are learning a language with a notebook.

A CAUTION ABOUT PREDICTION

Prediction leaves you open to making mistakes, and this is not always good for language learning. Furthermore, without someone or something to give you valuable feedback, you may not know if your predictions are accurate or not. Thus, we recommend that you use prediction on occasion, but not for every occasion. When there is a greater need for you to be accurate and precise with your language, there are other strategies that will serve you better.

SET A PERSONAL GOAL

Think of specific times in your future when you will want to predict. You might start with the phrase *I will predict when...*

Personal Goal for Practicing Prediction

EXPLORE STRATEGY 4

PREPARING

DEFINITION

Preparing is a skill that good language learners often use when they imagine future contexts. For example, language learners might be given an assignment in class to speak for five minutes about their families. These students will likely need to prepare ahead of time: perhaps by looking up unfamiliar vocabulary, creating an outline, and then rehearsing the speech to friends, family members, or even alone.

Preparing is, in a sense, an act of predicting itself, because fundamentally you are examining an unknown future situation, and doing your best to get ready for it. And remember that we are asking you to create a linguistic event every week or every month. It should come as no surprise that we believe in preparation!

STUDY AND STORY ON PREPARING

One illuminating study examined the coping strategies of English language learners at an American university (Leki, 1995). This particular study examined how language learners in a new culture, in this case the university culture, survive.

In the study, five language learners were interviewed and evaluated, and this resulted in the emergence of some very clear patterns. Among these patterns was the fact that international students in U.S. universities often do an astonishing amount of preparing (likely much more than American counterparts). Ling, for example, used past models to inform her writing, and prepared herself by consistently going to the library and reading books. She stated, "I am Chinese. I take advantage" (241). This phrase seems to suggest that her belief in preparing, studying, and putting in extra time would set her apart.

ADDITIONAL STUDY

How vital to success is the willingness to endure and prepare ahead of time? Consider this. A researcher at the University of Pennsylvania, Erling Boe, noticed an unusual trend when assessing math scores around the world. He noticed that students who did better on the test coincidentally were those who filled out the most questions on a rather lengthy questionnaire that accompanied the test. In fact, the correlation between the test and the seemingly "endless questionnaire" was so precise that the researcher stated that it was easy to predict which countries were best at math without even administering the test. The questionnaire, surprisingly, was enough.

How could a completely unrelated demographic questionnaire be related to math? Boe's conclusion was simple: effort and hard work were the key. Some cultures were simply more willing to fill out a tedious questionnaire than others, and that willingness to suffer through and stick to a task, even if you don't understand the importance of the task, ends up being essential. In other words, you could predict how good people are at math by "simply looking at which national cultures place the highest emphasis on effort and hard work" (adapted from Gladwell, 2008).

TRY IT OUT

Going on a vacation, attending a business meeting, or writing a letter in another language? All of these things require advanced planning and preparing. Consider the following techniques:

1. WRITING: Look up vocabulary, sample templates, or models of the kind of writing you want to do. Make an outline if necessary.
2. SPEAKING: Watch others speak on the same topic you want to speak on. Look for common phrases that you might need to use. Some speakers write out their speech in their native language first.
3. LISTENING AND READING: You have likely seen the person preparing for a trip to China by listening to Chinese language videos or reading a Chinese textbook on the plane. Please don't forget that much of your study is in preparation for a particular event that you are reaching for, and that exposure to a language is one of the best forms of preparation!

A CAUTION ON PREPARING

In the same study mentioned in our first story, another English language learner, Jien, often overestimated what was expected of her, and studied and prepared so much that a less than a perfect score on a subtask, was deflating to her.

So please recognize that while preparing ahead of time is a good idea, because preparing is an act of predicting, you can often overestimate or underestimate the amount of preparation you will need to accomplish the task in front of you.

SET A PERSONAL GOAL

Think of a task you want to accomplish. What do you need to do to prepare for it? You might start with the phrase *I'm preparing for…*

Personal Goal for Preparing

EXPLORE STRATEGY 5

PRACTICE AND PERFORM

DEFINITION

Most people would agree that practice is required when it comes to artistic skills such as playing the violin, athletic skills such as basketball, and even intellectual pursuits such as chess or backgammon. But for some reason, classroom instruction in language often limits the amount of time that students spend on practicing a language. In fact, it has often been lamented that teachers have "too little time" to have students practice, so the majority of time in class is spent on instruction.

Too little time to practice? Considering the importance of practice in developing linguistic skills, this educational lament is certainly antithetical to language gains. If you want to learn a language, practice should come first rather than last on the instructional totem pole.

STUDY AND STORY ON PRACTICE

A common story that is sometimes used to dismiss the importance of practice is that some people are just born with a gift of music, language, or any discipline. While there is no doubt that some people can excel at certain disciplines with LESS practice, even geniuses still have to put in the hard work to be good at them.

For example, in the book, *Genius Explained*, author Michael Howe demonstrates that Mozart had over 3,000 hours of piano practice....by the time he was six! And Daniel Coyle further explains in his 2009 book *The Talent Code* that people who are considered geniuses "typically accumulate massive amounts of prior exposure to those domains, through such means as listening to music in the home." He explains that deep practice, or the ability to pay special attention while exposed to a task, is something that these learners do as a matter of routine.

In other words, Mozart probably listened to music and noticed things you and I simply don't because he was constantly being taught to improve whatever he heard whenever he heard it. His brain was simply wired (and at an early age) to write and rewrite the language of music.

Now, applied to a language learner, what might that mean? Well, first of all, good language learners, just like Mozart, practice, and they practice a lot. But perhaps even more importantly, whenever they practice, great learners seek to improve what they know—they pay attention to the holes—the gaps in their knowledge—and to their ever-growing system of understanding. In other words, they don't just practice, they practice deeply. It might look like they are just gifted at learning a language, but the truth is, what they are doing even when it looks like they aren't doing anything is: practice!

TRY IT OUT

One of the best ways to engage in practice is to set boundaries or conditions around the practice time. Make sure you find a quiet place where you can get "lost" in the work you are doing. Athletes often refer to this as getting "in the zone." An additional discussion of "flow" and "getting in the zone" will be discussed later. For now, just remember that your job is not just to practice, but to get lost in deep practice. Here are some specific tips:

1. PRACTICE IN WRITING: Give yourself specific restraints when you write such as a particular time limit and a particular word count. Or write a paragraph using a list of words, a particular grammar tense, or other linguistic feature that you want to practice. Shakespeare used to practice the sonnet as a way to focus his ideas and intent in a particularly limited way: only 14 lines but I have to express a very difficult and complex thought? That fires up the motor cortex for sure!

2. PRACTICE IN LISTENING: While listening to a movie, song, video, or conversation, you might want to deepen your practice by listening for a particular linguistic feature, like verbs, or nouns, or past tense, or transitional phrases. Again, you might listen for a certain amount of time and then summarize that writing or recreate it. Dictation forces you to focus on language elements you might otherwise ignore, thus deepening your attention and your practice.

3. PRACTICE IN SPEAKING: A practice conversation or monologue might occur when you give yourself a specific list of words and speak using those words. Again, you might do this with a grammatical item, for example, speaking in past tense during a conversation,

or using commands. You might also choose a theme and speak only on that theme for a particular amount of time. Again, think of constraints yourself and then follow through with them.

4. PRACTICE IN READING: To practice with reading, you might choose a specific purpose in reading, such as reading for specific answers to questions, or identifying unknown words and guessing their meaning. You might also sometimes read for speed and focus solely on increasing how much you can read while maintaining understanding.

A CAUTION ON PRACTICE

Practice is often done in isolation, meaning it can be easier to do by yourself than with others. Performance, on the other hand, is your ability to put all that practice into action. You'll want to alternate between practice by yourself, and regular exposure and performing that language with others. For those of you familiar with the diffuse and focused modes of learning, this should resonate. Not familiar with the concepts? Go to our online course to learn more.

SET A PERSONAL GOAL

Think about how you can turn one of your activities on your weekly/monthly task sheet into an opportunity for practice!

Personal Goal for Practice	
Current Activity	Current Activity with Practice

INTROSPECT STRATEGY 1

MONITORING

DEFINITION

Monitoring is the ability to look at your own language before, during, or after you produce it. Have you ever stopped yourself before you spoke? Or perhaps you paid special attention to your accent or your grammar as you speak? Or perhaps you looked over something you wrote and noticed some mistakes? That, in essence, is *monitoring*.

According to Stephen Krashen, the purpose of learning (as opposed to acquiring) a language is to gain enough insight into language that you can self-correct. In other words, all that book studying, grammar studying, and rule studying CAN help you speak better, but only if you will use that knowledge to monitor your production.

STUDY ON MONITORING

In one revealing study, researchers Yule, Hoffman, and Damico (1987) noticed that students who were taught to monitor their own pronunciation actually became worse on a phoneme discrimination task (a pronunciation test). To some, this seemed to show that self-monitoring is a bad idea. But not so fast! Even though their pronunciation skills seemed to be deteriorating, in a follow up study it was discovered that over the long term, students who learned to monitor ended up being even better language learners compared to their peers.

In other words, in the short term, it seems that self-monitoring might inhibit you, even make you worse, but over time, those who pay special attention—monitor—their language, are "in a better position, when listening to a native speaker, to respond more quickly when they knew their [ability to hear sounds was] secure."

STORY ON MONITORING

One woman recounts a story of being a young child and being excited to record herself for the first time on a tape recorder. It was close to her fourth birthday. She exclaimed, "I just love birthday parties, parties!" When she heard herself on the recording, however, she was shocked to learn that she didn't say her "r's" at all, and it revealed that she said instead, "I just love birthday potties, potties." She simply didn't know she sounded like that and had never received any feedback to tell her differently.

TRY IT OUT

There are several simple ways to "monitor" your language. Here are a few:

1. Record yourself and pay attention to any errors you make. You might pay attention to vocabulary choice, verb conjugations, or pronunciation.

2. Prepare for conversations ahead of time. You might want to write things out and give yourself additional time to think about what you want to say and how to say it correctly.

3. While you are speaking, slow down when you arrive at a difficult language item. You may want to stop and ask for help, or take a note so that you can study more about that item later. In some sense, you are learning to have a conversation with yourself about language so that you can be more and more successful over time.

A CAUTION ON MONITORING

Thinking about your language while speaking it can sometimes be a real huge pain. It can slow you down and make you lose sight of what you are trying to communicate. Monitoring, while a useful skill, can sometimes be quite intrusive. This is probably why, in the research we presented, students did worse at the beginning.

You might think of it as correcting a swing of a bat in baseball or a racquet in tennis. If you have to change the way you naturally swing, it might make you worse at the beginning, but in the long term, a correct swing will help you out.

REFLECT ON MONITORING

Choose one of the activities prescribed in the TRY IT OUT section and apply it to one of the language tasks you have planned for this week/month.

How was monitoring successful for you?

INTROSPECT STRATEGY 2

JOURNALING

DEFINITION

Reflective journaling is the act of writing down your own learning experiences. It allows you to think back on and record your successes and failures as a language learner. It is then used as a way to adjust or improve upon your strategies.

STUDIES ON JOURNALING

Journaling is a technique found to increase one's health (Purcell, 2016), memory (Klein & Boals, 2001), and increases your ability to set and accomplish goals (Latham & Locke, 2007).

In one particular study, it was shown that the act of writing itself, rather than typing on a computer, actually improves learning as well. As Mueller and Oppenheimer (2014) suggest, "When people type their notes, they have this tendency to try to take verbatim notes and write down as much...as they can, [whereas those] who [take] longhand notes in our studies were forced to be more selective—because [they] can't write as fast as

[they] can type. And that extra processing of the material...bene-fited them."

What might this mean for language journaling? That the act of writing things down, while it may appear slow to some of you faster learners, may be a key to retaining what you learn.

TRY IT OUT

1. WRITE A SELF-REFLECTIVE JOURNAL. A self-reflective journal is basically an opportunity for you to examine how you are learning. Imagine, for example, that you are a scientist and you are basically recording how well you think you are doing in each experiment you choose. For example, after a particular experiment or goal, take some time to write what went well and what did not. You might want to consider the following questions to guide your journal entry. As you review these questions, you don't necessarily need to write about each question each time, rather use these questions to guide your thoughts:

- *What did I do well?*
- *What could I do better?*
- *What mistakes did I make?*
- *What was I very good at?*
- *What techniques did I use as I attempted to learn?*
- *What techniques did I enjoy?*

2. WRITE A PHRASE JOURNAL. A phrase journal is a collec-tion of common words and phrases that hasn't been assembled for you, rather you have sought them out because your conversa-tions and thoughts demand them. In other words, a phrase journal is a collection of the phrases YOU want to learn. A phrase journal is individual, and reflects your unique hobbies, thoughts, and conversational topics.

- *What do I want to be able to say?*
- *What are the phrases I will need next time I speak?*
- *If I imagine myself speaking with others, what would I like to always be able to say?*
- *What makes me unique? What words do I need to reflect that?*
- *What topics interest me? What do I want to learn that reflects those topics?*

A CAUTION ON JOURNALING

While it is often good to write down your thoughts, reflective journaling does not allow the kind of collaborative understanding that can come from a dialogue journal. On the other hand, sometimes it is difficult to find a partner that is willing to dialogue with you about your learning journey.

REFLECT ON JOURNALING

After completing a language activity, write about your experience using a reflective or dialogue journal. Then write down whether it was useful or not.

How was journaling successful for you?

INTROSPECT STRATEGY 3

THINK ALOUDS

DEFINITION

Think alouds are often used as research-collecting instruments among social scientists who are constantly trying to find out what people are thinking. However, we have also discovered that thinking aloud is useful for learners themselves, and not just the scientists. Thinking aloud, in a sense, allows you to be a scientist, talking to yourself and examining the reason you do things.

Think alouds can be especially useful when you are making plans, such as your weekly or monthly language plans, and can be used to help you examine your own strategies while you read a difficult passage.

For example, as you complete certain language tasks, talking out loud to yourself and answering the question *Why am I doing this?* can be very useful. It might sound strange, but sometimes talking out loud about **WHY** you are doing something can help give you insights you wouldn't otherwise have.

STUDY ON THINK ALOUD PROTOCOLS

Bereiter and Bird (1985) conducted two studies that demonstrated how think alouds helped a group of students read. Students were able to, after training, recognize and utilize strategies such as restatement, backtracking, recognizing a gap in understanding, and problem formation.

In other words, students became aware of their strategies and then used them more often simply by talking out loud about the passage they were reading.

TRY IT OUT

1. LANGUAGE PLAN THINK ALOUD: While you create your language plan, talk out loud about WHY you are choosing the activities you are choosing. As you move to create different activities, share what benefit you think each activity will have. You might also think out loud after seeing the results of your language plan, and reason through what you think worked well and what did not.

2. READING COMPREHENSION THINK ALOUD: While you read an article or passage, talk to yourself about what you are doing. Consider the following phrases:

- *Okay, now I am going to read the first paragraph.*
- *Wait, I didn't understand that. Let me go back.*
- *What could that mean? I think I should circle that word.*
- *That doesn't make sense yet. I think the story will explain later.*
- *I can't figure this out. I think I need to do something. Maybe I can…*

A CAUTION ON THINK ALOUDS

Think alouds can sometimes be uncomfortable for people who are not accustomed to them. Some people think that it makes them look weird or even crazy, and there may be places (such as a library) where a think aloud doesn't make much sense at all.

Additionally, think alouds can sometimes get in the way of your learning rather than help it out, so this method shouldn't be used in every situation. Can you imagine using a think aloud when trying to have a dinner conversation? *I think I'll try to ask for the potatoes. Excuse me, sir, may I have some potatoes?*

REFLECT ON THINK ALOUDS

Consider using a language plan think aloud or a reading comprehension think aloud. Write down how you think it went.

How was using a think aloud successful for you?

INTROSPECT STRATEGY 4

SOCIAL AWARENESS STRATEGIES

DEFINITION

What is a social awareness strategy? While it might be defined any number of ways, such a strategy means that you, as a learner, have figured something out about the culture or society. Social awareness means that you can understand social cues such as when to speak, when to remain silent, what is considered an appropriate conversation piece, and when to laugh. It might include how close to get to someone while speaking, how to dress, and how to ask for help.

Sometimes rules of social awareness are only made obvious to you when you break the rule. You may have heard that it is polite to burp after a meal in some countries. You may have heard not to talk about politics in some countries, but then when you arrive, you are asked several questions about politics. Now what?

SITUATIONS FOR SOCIAL AWARENESS STRATEGIES: WHAT WOULD YOU DO?

Read the following social situations and consider what you might do for each.

1. You are in a group of native speakers and suddenly they all break into laughter. You have no idea what was just said.
2. You are given a gift from a native speaker. You have no gift and want to respond politely.
3. You have just spoken to a group of people using your best language skills, but they stare at you, frowning slightly.
4. You are in a group conversation. Moments ago you made a mistake, and you realize it just now. What do you do?

TRY IT OUT

1. CONDUCT A SOCIAL SURVEY: Find a native speaker or someone who has visited the country of your choice and ask the following questions:

- What is considered "rude" in the culture?
- What mistakes do foreigners sometimes make?
- What makes the culture unique?
- How can I be polite in the culture?
- What do I say (and do) when I don't understand what is happening?

2. PRACTICE PHRASES FOR REQUESTS AND CLAR-IFICATION: Find out how to say and practice the following (phrases will differ slightly from language to language):

- *Could you repeat that?*
- *How do you say that?*
- *I'm sorry, I don't understand.*

3. PRACTICE PHRASES FOR REPAIR

Find out how to say and practice the following (phrases will differ slightly from language to language):

- *Oh. I meant to say…*
- *I'm sorry. I made a mistake.*
- *Did I make a mistake? What did I say?*
- *Could you help me? I think I'm saying this wrong.*

A CAUTION ON SOCIAL AWARENESS STRATEGIES

There are thousands of ways to make mistakes, and even in your own native culture, you run the risk of offending others or making an occasional blunder. One of the best pieces of advice we can give you is this simple shield against embarrassment: learn to laugh at yourself, and know that you are not alone.

SET A PERSONAL GOAL

Share a cultural blunder! Everyone makes mistakes when learning another language. Have you or someone else made a social mistake that you can share?

What social mistakes have you or others made?

FLEXIBILITY STRATEGY 1

RECOMBINATION

DEFINITION

If you were given 50 words from an unknown language, would you be able to create sentences out of those 50 words? With just those few words, do you believe you could you create something interesting? Perhaps a poem? A request? A statement of fact? If you said yes to any of these, you may be the kind of language architect that is interested in the art of recombination.

Recombination is a technique preferred by learners who love to "play" with language. In short, recombination refers to the rearranging of the pieces of language. If you think of words as building blocks, then recombination is the practice of taking those building blocks and creating something new out of them.

Recombination is in full force when you rephrase or simplify. Teachers will often ask you to "state in your own words," or "find another way to say" something. These are invitations to recombine, and are an essential way to help learners use the limited words they have to express meaning.

Recombining is a useful technique when you get caught

midsentence and don't know a word in the target language. This will force you to find a different way to say the same thing. Recombining is also useful for taking words you have just learned and applying them to current or future conversations.

STUDY AND MORE ON RECOMBINATION

While languages often have upwards of 200,000 words or more, how many words does one need to know to be functional or fluent? Because these terms are interpreted in a lot of different ways, answers vary, however, researchers tend to believe that with vocabulary sizes of just 3,000 words, most people can understand about 95% of language (Hazenberg and Hulstijn, 1996).

Does that mean you need 3,000 words to express yourself, however? A number of researchers believe that while you need 3,000-5,000 words to understand most ideas, with even fewer words you can express quite a lot. In fact, if you are astrophysicist Roberto Trotta, you might be able to express the entire history of the universe in 1,000 words. Trotta (2014), partially in reaction to his colleague's use of ridiculously difficult jargon and partially because he loves fun, created a "history of the universe as we know it" using only the 1,000 most common English words.

TRY IT OUT

1. READING: After reading an article or story, take 10 unfamiliar words with you that day (bring a notebook). Use those words in your speaking or written communication.
2. PARAPHRASING PRACTICE: As you read or listen, take a sentence or phrase and try to make it your own. This is often best done by listening to the

phrase several times, and then asking yourself how YOU would say it.

3. SUMMARIZING THE CINEMA: After watching a show or movie, spend time explaining the plot of that show in a short summary to a friend.

4. WHAT I MEAN IS: With a partner or group, try to come up with a sentence and see how many ways you can say the same thing. Use the phrase *What I mean is...* each time you come up with a new, original way of saying the same thing. This game can be especially fun in large groups.

A CAUTION ON RECOMBINATION

You should not be surprised to find that, as you recombine, and especially speaking with someone in real time, you might lose some of the original meaning of what you were trying to say. Some of our greatest mistakes have come because we tried to express meanings using new words, but we didn't understand exactly what that word meant. However, that is why the next strategy, hedging and repairing, becomes so useful. If you risk too much and make a mistake? What do you do to fix a mistake?

SET A PERSONAL GOAL

Consider one of the four activities above and apply it to your language learning task for this week/month.

Which of the recombination strategies did you choose? How did it work?

FLEXIBILITY STRATEGY 2

HEDGING AND REPAIRING

DEFINITION

What do you do when you don't speak a language well, but you still want to give it a try? You hedge and repair, that's what! Hedging refers to the strategy of communicating uncertainty or caution to a listener, signaling to the listener a need for empathy or even help.

Repairing often follows...this is the strategy of improving your speech so that it meets the needs of the listener. After you hedge a speech, you often invite a listener to help you repair it.

STORY ON HEDGING AND REPAIRING

Language learners often undergo a certain psychological transformation with regards to a second or third language.

One Spanish learner mused, "I'm just nicer in Spanish. My friend pointed it out to me. He said that I almost switch personalities. And I suppose that's true, in a way. In my native language, I am dominant and confident. I can say whatever I need to rather easily. However, when I speak my second language, I am shy and a bit more uncertain. Much of this is unconscious, but some of it, to be honest, is strategy. I need others to help me out when I say the wrong word. I need others to forgive me for my accent when it gets in the way. I send out signals to help listeners know that I am not completely in control, and that they are free to interrupt me, correct me, or just help me out. I always show appreciation. I can't imagine ever feeling the same way about my native language. If someone tried to correct my grammar, I'd probably be ticked off."

TRY IT OUT

1. HEDGE WITH PHRASES: TRANSLATE AND THEN PRACTICE THESE PHRASES IN YOUR TARGET LANGUAGE:

- *I'm sorry, I'm just learning*
- *My French/Chinese/Arabic isn't very good yet*
- *I am looking for the right word*
- *I can't say this well.*
- *I think the word is X.*

2. HEDGE WITH YOUR VOICE AND BODY. When people hedge, or show uncertainty, they often use "filler words." See if you can research the filler words from your target language. In English, we often use fillers such as *um, uh,* and *well.* You'll notice we slow down and change our tone also when we are trying to show uncertainty. Your body language also can show uncertainty. In most cultures, raising your eyes to look anxious and attentive is important. Sometimes scratching your head or scrunching your eyebrows helps.

3. REPAIR WITH PHRASES:

- *I'm sorry. I meant to say…*
- *What I mean is…*
- *I don't know how to say this. I'll try to say it again.*

4. REPAIR BY INVITING A NEGOTIATION.

When people repair, they often elicit the help of others to do so. Can you think of ways you can invite others to correct you?

- *Could you help me?*
- *How do you say X?*
- *What is the word that means X?*

5. SHOWING GRATITUDE.

Finally, it is important to show gratitude when others help you repair your language. Gratitude can be shown in your body language, tone, and again, in the words you use. Don't forget to say thank you to those that help out.

A CAUTION ON HEDGING AND REPAIRING

Some people just don't like to make mistakes in front of others. It is certainly difficult to feel like a child, so to speak, when you cannot communicate your thoughts as freely as you can in your native language. This psychosocial phenomenon often makes it so that learners refuse to engage with others.

Truth be told, sometimes hedging and repairing may make you appear different from who you really are. However, that is why we have placed these two strategies in the chapter about flexibility. Can you do something uncomfortable? Can you appear like a child even though you are quite bright? Will you ask for help from others?

SET A PERSONAL GOAL

Consider one of the five activities above and apply it to your language learning task for this week/month.

Which of the five activities did you choose? How did it work?

FLEXIBILITY STRATEGY 3

CULLING FOR ANSWERS

DEFINITION AND STORY

Student: *Teacher, what does environment mean?*
Teacher: *It means where you are.*
Student (to another): *Environment means Mexico.*

When you need to understand a definition of a word you don't know, what do you do? Let's imagine that you usually ask a teacher for the answer. What if the teacher is unavailable—maybe talking to another student? Do you simply resign yourself to the idea that you'll never learn that word, or do you search out different resources?

When you do finally get an answer (let's say your teacher finally becomes available and gives you a quick answer), do you simply accept the answer as the truth and move on, or do you seek for confirmation that the answer was correct?

You see, language learners often need to seek for answers to understand things, and the best language learners often don't stop after a failed attempt at getting information. Good language learners will use a teacher, a student in class, a parent, an online dictionary, a textbook, and many other resources to find the answers to their questions. They're tireless.

But that's not all. Good language learners also realize that not every explanation is equal to another. If your teacher is in a hurry, the answer to the definition may not be very good or very clear. Often teachers and dictionaries provide just one-word synonyms when students ask the meaning of a word, and students who rely on just single word answers to new words do so at their peril.

Let's imagine a teacher says that the word *toxic* means *poisonous*. Pretty good, right? However, the word *toxic* isn't exactly the same as poisonous, is it? To illustrate, if I said *Those snakes are toxic* or *There are barrels of poisonous waste*, you would probably think something felt a little wrong. We say *poisonous snakes* and *toxic waste*, don't we? The simple explanation that *toxic* = *poisonous* is imperfect.

Imperfect explanations like these are also common when we search for answers to grammatical principles. Often, learners receive a single or simplistic answer to a grammar principle (you don't pronounce the *s* at the end of words in French) only to learn that there are myriad exceptions to the rule.

The vocabulary word *cull* (to gather or collect) has an interesting connotation. It doesn't just mean to gather, but also to eliminate wrong choices or imperfect information. Language learners that cull information not only try to find answers in a variety of ways, but they also tend to gather a variety of answers, looking for and implementing which answers are best, and revising or completely discarding answers which may not be as accurate.

By the way…why don't we say *toxic snakes* or *poisonous waste* in English? One simple answer is that we tend to reserve the word *toxic* for non-living substances, and we reserve *poisonous* more often for animals and plant. But don't take our word for it. Keep culling.

TRY IT OUT

1. SURVEY THE CROWD. Rather than asking one person about a particular question, try to survey a variety of people. As you do, you might want to consider asking them about the rule or word you want to know about, but how they would use it in context. Facebook, Twitter, and other social media sites provide a great opportunity for people to post their own definitions or explanations. Ask a question and see how many different responses you get.

2. LABEL AND ORDER THE RESOURCE: When you have a question, think quickly about how you might generally go about answering that question. Then think of other ways of finding an answer to the question. Think of as many ways as possible to get an answer to your question. Then order your list from *most reliable resource* to *least reliable resource*.

3. WORD SCAVENGER HUNT: Go online and find out how people use a word. Type the word into a search engine and see how the word is actually used in sentences. Some specialized websites called "online corpora" can help you search how words are used among a large number of speakers. It can be addicting to see how words change over time, and an online word corpus might be just the thing for those of you that like to see lots of examples.

A CAUTION ON CULLING

As with so many self-directed efforts, when you try to cull for information, you can often be wrong. You might choose one answer as better than another, only to discover that you have chosen incorrectly. However, culling is a skill that should keep a learner constantly revising their understanding of language rules, so when you find out that your current framework is wrong, as a good language learner, you simply revise it. Another way to say this is that, those who are good at culling never truly stop; rather, they just keep revising.

SET A PERSONAL GOAL

Consider one of the four activities above and apply it to your language learning task for this week/month.

Which of the four activities did you choose? How did it work?

FLEXIBILITY STRATEGY 4

GOAL SETTING

DEFINITION

Goal setting is definitely a strategy that language learners use in order to demonstrate their flexibility. Setting goals could be both long term and short term, but often demonstrate a learner's willingness to stretch and do things that are uncomfortable and ambitious. Learners who set goals tend to focus more on their desired outcome then the difficulties they face.

STUDY ON GOAL SETTING

In one study (Yang 1998) on language learner autonomy, a researcher had students study several chapters on language learning strategies. They also discussed their own special tricks to learn a language. Then the researcher asked students to set their own goals, and followed up with those goals in a weekly diary. At the end of the course, the students shared the results.

And what were the results? The researcher found that students not only improved their use of language learner strategies but gained insights into their own personalities and were motivated by their ability to measure their own progress.

TRY IT OUT

You may have noticed that this entire book is a reminder of the importance of goal setting in language learning. Make sure you keep up your weekly/monthly tasks, and do all you can to reflect on your own learning.

A CAUTION ON GOAL SETTING

Is anything wrong with goal setting? Well, perhaps not, but it is true that some learners have difficulty following up with their goals, and when they cannot keep up their goals, become demotivated and depressed. One way to overcome this natural inclination to get depressed is to have a "short memory," meaning you need to forget past goals and focus on new ones. By seeing failure as a common event rather than as an indication of your own identity, language learners can maintain their enthusiasm.

In other words, give yourself a break! When one strategy doesn't work, try another! When one plan doesn't work, adjust and try again. When you fail to accomplish what you set out to do, try again. In something as lifelong as language learning, rather than being obsessed with the results, why not be fascinated with the process? Now, how flexible is that?

SET A PERSONAL GOAL

Take some time to think, reflect, and then write about your goals.

Review your long-term and short-term goals.
Which goal excites you most, and why?

DETAILS STRATEGY 1

DEEP PRACTICE

DEFINITION

Deep practice is a technique wherein you focus in on the details of something in order to master it. It might be a small musical phrase for a musician, or a single move in basketball. In language, deep practice refers to identifying a form and seeking to master that form. The form might be grammatical, lexical, or auditory. A learner often identifies an error or difficulty, and then works on it through a series of steps.

Daniel Coyle, *New York Times* best-selling author, identified several steps to create a deep practice session:

Step 1: **ABSORB THE WHOLE.** The first step is to try to understand the whole of the skill you are hoping to master.

Step 2: **BREAK IT INTO CHUNKS.** This is often the work that teachers do to help students understand something. A teacher, when giving you something beyond your level of ability, often tries to break down the different components of something so that you can better understand it. For example, if you were learning music with three difficult rhythms, the teacher might take each of these three rhythms and work on them separately. The idea behind separating out difficult bits of information is that, in isolation, you can target them with more frequency and focus. You are then more likely to perform the action fluidly and automatically.

Step 3: SLOW IT DOWN AND REPEAT. After identifying the different steps or chunks, the next step is to slow down each chunk, one by one, and then, gradually, as you master each chunk, you can repeat it at a faster rate.

Step 4: FEEL IT. Finally, you can go back to absorbing the entire whole of the skill again. Return to it and see how the chunks fit together. Often, this involves visualization. For learners of language, "feeling the whole" also means that when you hear something that is not correct, it feels incorrect. Some might suggest, in fact, that it should bother you, like a musician who hears a wrong note. When you can hear correct and incorrect language forms, an action often referred to as "noticing," you will have gained a valuable skill to help you monitor your own learning progress.

(From Daniel Coyle, *The Talent Code*, 2009)

STUDY AND STORY ON DEEP PRACTICE

Would you be surprised to know that studying an article once and testing yourself on it four times is *better* than reading the article four times and testing yourself once?

If you think about what we have already taught you, perhaps you can understand why that would be so. An active task approach (our very first principle) teaches us that it is much better to struggle with a task, be actively engaged in it, rather than just studying a lot before an exam. There is a level of intensity and focus that comes with a testing environment, and being willing to be put under the lens of scrutiny. Furthermore, in testing circumstances, by paying attention to errors you receive the feedback necessary to make changes.

In other words, if you want to learn a language, making a lot of mistakes and paying attention to those mistakes makes a big difference.

TRY IT OUT

1. DEEP PRACTICE READING

1. Read an article, passage, or other material. Choose something that is just above your level of comprehension.
2. Chunk it. Divide the passage into logical pieces. It might be sentences, paragraphs, chapters, or some other way of categorizing it.
3. Figure each part out. Spend time looking at each piece separately. Ask questions to yourself about it. Use all of the techniques you have learned to understand the meaning of the words, phrases, and general concepts.
4. Read it again and *feel* it. Read the article again. This time, try summarizing in a think-aloud activity, think of how each section connects to the other and write a small summary to see if you can capture the main ideas.

2. DEEP PRACTICE LISTENING

1. Watch the movie, show, or other listening material. Choose something that is just above your level of comprehension.
2. Listen in chunks. Divide the material into roughly three parts, or find natural breaks (changes in scene or topic) for the breaks to occur. Now listen to each portion separately. Take notes for each of the breaks. Stop at unfamiliar words or phrases. Use all the techniques you can to understand it. For example, you might practice phrases out loud so that you can understand and use them. You might use subtitles and a dictionary. When possible, interact with others and ask questions.
3. Listen again and *feel* it. You may wish to summarize the listening material after listening to it again. Spend time with phrases that are difficult until they feel fluid. One fun tip is to summarize as if you were narrating the listening material as a movie narrator.

3. DEEP PRACTICE WRITING AND SPEAKING

1. When attempting to use deep practice in writing and speaking, you might want to look at the writing process itself as an attempt to chunk. Consider the following commonly reported techniques for process writing:
2. Think of the whole and divide into chunks: Create an outline.
3. Review each chunk separately and slow it down: Create successive drafts and add details. Review each section and give each section adequate support.

4. Feel it: In your 3rd draft, read it out loud, read it to others, and change what still feels awkward.

4. DEEP PRACTICE WITH GRAMMAR, PRONUNCIATION, OR A GENERAL FOCUS ON FORM

1. Absorb the whole. Find a form that you struggle with. Listen to it repeatedly. Find multiple examples of it. Find instruction on it.
2. Chunk it up. Good instruction will often help you see how to chunk the form adequately. If no instruction can be found, you may have to try to chunk it yourself. For example, you may have to ask yourself some basic questions such as: what are the basic rules of this form? How is it created? How is it different from other forms? When is this form used?
3. Slow it down. Try out the form. You may find practice exercises readily available online and in other materials to help you.
4. Repeat it. Try the form successively over a period of time. The difficulty of the form will determine the amount of time spent.
5. Feel it. You should be able to recognize the form when you hear and read the language you are studying. If the form is used incorrectly, it should feel strange/wrong to you. You should be able to recall the form when it comes up in your own speaking or writing.

A CAUTION ON DEEP PRACTICE

Deep practice is a technique that is widely applied to a number of different scenarios. Theorists of language learning are quick to point out that language may be different than learning math, history, or other material. Since the goal is acquisition, not just rote memory or learning, then techniques that focus on memory may fade quickly when not applied over time. Thus, it is quite likely that forms studied can quickly be forgotten if no longer seen.

SET A PERSONAL GOAL

Make a list of forms in the language you are working on. You might find a list of beginning, intermediate, or advanced forms online. Consider which forms you would like to work on. This might come from considerations of frequency (*How often I am seeing this form in my daily study?*) or difficulty (*I keep making mistakes on this form*). Work to master these forms as part of your daily habits. You may want to receive feedback from a community to measure your progress.

Make a list of forms you are working on.

DETAILS STRATEGY 2

POMODORO: A FOCUS ON FOCUS

DEFINITION

A Pomodoro is a technique to eliminate distraction and to create hyperfocus on a topic. The concept of a Pomodoro was popularized by Francesco Cirillo in the late 1980s, and consisted of using a timer to break down work, most traditionally into 25 minute intervals. (Pomodoro means "tomato," which was said to be the shape of the timer Cirillo had as a university student.)

Put simply, the idea of a Pomodoro is to set aside all tasks, put on a timer, and for 25 minutes, work feverishly on that task alone. This means that, during the 25 minutes spent, a person using the Pomodoro technique will not use cellphones, email, social media, conversation, food, or any other distractions from interfering with the task at hand (this may mean either working in a place that allows that kind of privacy, or creating a place inside your head that allows you to focus amidst distraction).

A NOTE ABOUT PROCRASTINATION

Distraction is often seen as one of the greatest inhibitors of success. Studies on procrastination often show that distraction and anxiety often limit someone from beginning a task, but that once in the task, the feelings or anxiety can go away. What does this mean? It means that once you can get over the original difficulty of starting most tasks, the most uncomfortable part of the task is over with. It might sound strange at first, but it is nonetheless true that the most difficult part of many tasks is just beginning.

TRY IT OUT: THE BASIC POMODORO

1. Decide on the task to be done.
2. Set the Pomodoro timer (traditionally to 25 minutes).
3. Work on the task until the timer rings.
4. After the timer rings, put a checkmark on a piece of paper.
5. If you have fewer than four checkmarks, take a short break (3–5 minutes), then go to step 2.
6. After four Pomodoros, take a longer break (15–30 minutes), reset your checkmark count to zero, then go to step 1.

A CAUTION ON POMODOROS

While it is good to avoid distractions in order to increase work productivity, sometimes distractions may be of benefit to the workplace and to your study. Consider that not all distractions are of equal weight in the language learning world. For example, did you notice that Francois Gouin avoided the distraction of conversation partners in order to memorize language bits?

SET A PERSONAL GOAL

When focusing on form especially, consider using the Pomodoro technique to maximize the time and to limit the amount of distraction.

Try a Pomodoro sometime this week. How did it work?

DETAILS STRATEGY 3

SELECTIVE ATTENTION

DEFINITION

Selective attention comes from a theory that, at times, educators must point out certain features of language to students in order to help those students acquire them. Educators, in this sense, invited students to notice certain grammatical forms in otherwise authentic material.

This led to the idea that you could expose learners to a number of these forms in order for them to first notice the form, then learn about the form, and then finally, acquire the form. The concept of an "input flood" was developed to demonstrate that a teacher might choose or create material that had a large number of these forms. For example, an educator might choose the song *Hoping and Wishing* in order to demonstrate the different uses of gerunds in English.

STUDIES ON SELECTIVE ATTENTION

A number of theorists have discussed the importance of having students notice a feature in order for them to acquire it. It appears almost entirely impossible for learners to pick up on certain features unless they are exposed and made aware of them.

Richard Schmidt (1990) argues that an important part of language acquisition is noticing something consciously, and while that is in contrast with Stephen Krashen's view that learning something simply *isn't* the same as acquiring it, Lightbown (1985) suggests that perhaps formal instruction can create "hooks, points of access" because learners can notice something new that they didn't before.

TRY IT OUT

As language learners, once again, to use this technique you will have to be your own instructor. This means that you will have to carefully look for forms that you are just beginning to notice. If you are unaware of certain features in language, you may want to spend time taking tests or quizzes and see where you may need additional focus on form.

Selective attention should also mean that, while you may make errors in other areas, your focus is turned away from those errors (at least for a time) as you work on improving just a single skill. Thus, you may look only at verb conjugation, for example, one week, and then spend time on phrasal verbs the next week. In other words, you selectively pay attention to certain forms, at your own choice, and then pay attention to another form later on.

A CAUTION ON SELECTIVE ATTENTION

Selective attention is something that trained professional language teachers often get a sense of over a long period of time. They can, in some sense and in varying degrees, know when a student is developmentally ready for certain language features. Manfred Pienemann (1998) suggested that there are certain language stages or features that should or can be taught in a particular order.

While trained professionals may have a better sense than you do about what you are ready to learn, every language learner should feel able and willing to do some self-evaluation and see if certain forms are within reach or not.

SET A PERSONAL GOAL

Select a language form that you believe is just beyond your reach. To do so, consider the following:

1. Are you starting to see this form in your daily reading/listening of your study?
2. Are you able to find quizzes or information about the language form?
3. Is there anyone who might help you with what this form should look like to give you the necessary feedback?

What phrases or structures are you noticing
this week that you haven't noticed in the past?

MEANING STRATEGY 1

FINDING FLOW

DEFINITION

Flow refers to the phenomenon of getting lost in a task. People who are in a state of "flow" are said to have higher focus, intensity, and performance. In terms of language learning, those who are in a state of flow are often intensely focused on language such as completing a communicative task or applying a grammatical principle.

STUDY AND STORY ON FLOW

H. Douglas Brown (2002) describes flow in language using the metaphor of playing tennis. He states that often if he thinks too much about all of the rules of tennis (where to swing a racket, where to place his feet), he can actually perform worse. He suggests taking an approach where you let the game come to you; or, in other words, relax and focus on the main purpose of the game. By focusing on the main purpose (have fun and win), you simplify your path to success.

Translating this metaphor to language, we might state that your major goal each time you step on the language court is to have fun and communicate, and everything else you are doing should be reduced to that simple fact.

TRY IT OUT

1. SIMPLIFYING THE PROCESS: One way to get into a flow state, especially when studying, is to take away all distractions. Turn off your phone, turn off the TV, and pay attention directly to what you are studying. It is often best to consider having a very direct goal, something that is terribly simple to remember (*I am going to memorize 50 words in the next 20 minutes; I am going to write without interruptions an entire page*).

2. MANTRAS TO THINK ABOUT: Some people often find a better state of flow simply by telling themselves basic truths. For example, telling yourself your goal or outcome, and saying it out loud, is often very useful. Here are some other mantras people have found useful:

- *Nothing else exists right now. Only this task.*
- *I can find a way to solve this task. I can do this.*
- *I see myself succeeding. I can see myself speaking perfectly.*

3. FOCUS ON MEANING: While there are many rules in language to focus on, ultimately, when you are trying to communicate, you may find that a focus on too many things is distracting. Thus, for many people, you must find moments where you are only focusing on getting your message across and having a good time. Remember, language is supposed to be fun and supposed to connect you with others. Make sure you have

moments where you aren't just practicing language through study, you are actually playing the game.

4. INCREASING INTENSITY: Another way to get into a flow state is to increase the intensity of your activity. If you are listening to a movie, consider increasing the difficulty by telling yourself that you want to identify 10 verbs you didn't know before. If you are having a conversation, consider using new words you wrote previously in your notebook. Having a particular focus often gives you greater results and can make the drudgery of an activity you are doing all the time a bit more fun.

A CAUTION ON FINDING FLOW

There is a great debate among teachers on whether to focus on grammar or focus on meaning. At one extreme, teachers who focus on meaning are often accused of ignoring grammar entirely, just letting students talk and listen to whatever they want. At another extreme, teachers who focus entirely on grammar are often accused of talking a lot about language, but never actually having students practice themselves.

It is obvious that a balance is needed, and whichever camp you find yourself in, flow is important. You see, flow can happen with either a focus on grammar or a focus on meaning. Since both modes are important to learning, alternating between a focus on grammar and a focus on meaning, and finding flow within both forms of study, is advised.

SET A PERSONAL GOAL

Consider one of the four activities above and apply it to your language learning task for this week/month.

Which of the four activities did you choose? How did it work?

MEANING STRATEGY 2

BE RESOURCEFUL THROUGH GROUP WORK

DEFINITION

Another way to increase risk and therefore need is by meeting in groups. You will find that communicating and working in a group heightens your focus and forces you to recall items you have studied, and even helps you to think of things you have never studied.

Group work can help you become more resourceful by making you think of ways to communicate your message that you never would have thought of otherwise.

STUDIES ON GROUP WORK

Should you be working with someone who is smarter than you at the language you are studying? Consider. One of the seminal studies of its day, Michael Long and other researchers (1976) determined that students produced greater quantity and quality of speech when working in groups rather than working with teacher-centered activities.

And in 1985, Long and Porter followed up this study by

giving us insights about whom you should study with. This time, he had learners work in groups with three kinds of partners: intermediate, advanced, or native-language partners. Long here discovered that learners produced the same quality of language regardless of the kind of partner they had, but that having a partner that was just above their skill level produced the most speech.

Yule and MacDonald (1990) demonstrated that in pairs, giving the learner with the least amount of language ability the harder task often created more negotiation and a greater variety of interaction.

In other words, find someone who knows more of the language than you, but make sure you take the harder role of communicating a message. They will often encourage you and elicit the best from you.

TRY IT OUT

1. BE THE SENDER: Try communicating a message that you care about. It could be a discussion about your family, your work, or your hobbies. It could be a personal philosophy that matters a lot to you. As you communicate your message, think of any and all ways you could make the message clear including: writing down words, drawing pictures, miming out action, repeating ideas.

2. BE THE RECEIVER: Listen to a message carefully and do all you can to try to understand the message. As you listen, help the sender by doing the following: repeating to check for understanding, asking questions, helping the sender find a word.

A CAUTION ON BEING RESOURCEFUL THROUGH GROUP WORK

While it is true that being resourceful is a skill worthy of your attention, sometimes you will lack the resources necessary to be clear. You may not have a dictionary, paper and pencil, or a smartphone to help you out. We always recommend that, especially when traveling, you think about all the resources you might want or need, and carry them with you as often as you can. You simply never know when you might need extra help!

SET A PERSONAL GOAL

Create a list of people who you think are candidates that might help you study your language. Then think about who might know just a bit more than you. These are often your best study partners.

Create a list of people who might help you study.
Write down what makes each person a good candidate.

MEANING STRATEGY 3

LET THE FIELD LIE FALLOW

DEFINITION

The idiomatic expression *Let the field lie fallow* refers to the idea that farmers would sometimes need to let a field rest for a season in order for the minerals in the soil to be replenished.

In language learning, this refers to the need for people to sometimes let their brain take breaks by doing something different. Can you get burned out on language learning? Absolutely, and that can affect your desire and your productivity. Here we give you a few tips for letting your brain relax.

STUDY AND STORY ON THE DIFFUSE MODE OF LEARNING

How do people learn language, or learn anything, really? Barbara Oakley suggests that there are two main ways, or modes of learning. She calls them the focused and diffuse modes of learning. The focused mode refers to an intense, very detail orientated way of learning. While we have been discussing a lot of very focused and intense techniques so far in this chapter, we want you to consider for a moment doing things in a diffuse, relaxed, manner.

Why would you want to relax as you learn? Well, according to a number of cognitive scientists and learning experts like Barbara Oakley (2013), it gives you a chance to make connections and productive in ways you wouldn't be otherwise.

Oakley describes these two different modes of learning by using the metaphor of a pinball machine. In one machine, the nobs are tightly packed, and so the pinball (your train of thought) hits the nobs most often that are nearest each other. In another machine, the nobs are loosely placed, so it is possible for your brain to make connections it never otherwise would have.

In other words, if you study in just one area of learning (say, just vocabulary for hours at a time), it can actually inhibit your ability to process information. You're not letting the information breathe. But if you will vary the types of activities and the ways in which you go about learning them, they are more likely to be recalled.

TRY IT OUT

There are a number of ways to move from an intense, focused approach toward a more diffuse one. Here are a few:

1. EXERCISE. Several studies have shown that exercising before you study can help get your brain thinking and moving just a bit better. You may even want to take a break during a large study session and do a little exercise in between.
2. IMAGINE. When you are writing or speaking, sometimes it is good to simply relax, stop staring at your screen, and just think. Allow your mind to wander. Imagine that you are talking to a celebrity, or

imagine speaking in front of thousands of cheering fans. A relaxed state of mind, one that allows you to be free in your thinking, can often give you fantastic results.

3. RELAXED LISTENING: Learning a language should be fun. Thus, while there should definitely be moments of intense study, there should also be moments when you are just enjoying language itself. Turn on a favorite movie and watch it in the language of your choice. Listen to music in the car. Listen to a radio show without taking notes or being intense about it.

4. DO SOMETHING ENTIRELY DIFFERENT: Good language learners are often good at OTHER things. When you find that you feel heavy or tired from a particular activity, vary that activity with something different or new. If you are focused on studying a grammar principle, try reading a book instead. If you are focused on listening to a news program, try reading a children's book. Try to find activities that complement each other. Sick of listening? Try writing. Sick of writing? Try speaking. Sick of speaking? Try reading. Sick of learning Chinese? Do a French language lesson. Sick of learning languages? Try singing, going on a hike, or painting.

5. SUGGESTOPEDIA: In the 1970's, a language learning method called Suggestopedia demonstrated that lowering someone's anxiety often made them better at learning a language. Suggestopedia proponents suggested making classrooms calming environments, with proper music, lighting, colors, to "set the mood." It was as relaxing an environment as you'll find in language learning. Want to get groovy

and relax yourself into learning? Try a few principles of Suggestopedia. Turn on relaxing music as you study, have a favorite snack nearby (how about a relaxing chamomile tea?), and do anything else you can think of to make the experience a relaxing one. One learner swore by yoga breathing and stretching. Sounds silly? That's part of the point...letting the field lie fallow means trying something new to break routine and let your brain think in unexpected ways.

A CAUTION ON LETTING THE FIELD LIE FALLOW

Some scholars believe that a relaxed approach to language learning, one in which a learner decides what to be exposed to, may lead to fossilization.

There are many cases of adults who have learned language to a certain point, but then simply stop progressing. Theorists speculate that these learners often focus on just being understood, and thus, they don't notice errors in grammar, pronunciation, or vocabulary.

When we suggest that you let the field lie fallow, we are not suggesting this as a proper course of action always, but rather that it is an important possibility to help make learning more enjoyable.

SET A PERSONAL GOAL

Consider one of the five activities above and apply it to your language learning task for this week/month.

Which of the five activities did you choose? How did it work?

REFERENCES

Acredolo, L.P., Goodwyn, S.W., Horobin, K. & Emmons, Y. (1999). The signs and sounds of early language development. In L. Balter & C. Tamis-LeMonda (Eds.) *Child Psychology* (pp.116–139). New York: Psychology Press.

Atkins, J. (2016). *Tell your research using only the 1000 most common words: Scicomm at ESA 2016.* Plos Blog Network. http://blogs.plos.org/blog/2016/08/27/science-communication-simple-words-and-story-telling-at-esa-2016/

Bereiter, C., & Bird, M. (1985). *Use of thinking aloud in identification and teaching of reading comprehension strategies.* Cognition and Instruction, 2, 131-156.

Brown, H. D. (2002) *Strategies for Success: A Practical Guide to Learning English,* White Plains, Longman.

Canale, M. and Swain, M. (1980) "Theoretical bases of communicative approaches to second language teaching and testing." *Applied Linguistics*, 1(1): 1-47.

Capirci, O. Cattani, A, Rossini, P. Volterra, V. (1998). Teaching sign language to hearing children as a possible factor in cognitive enhancement. J Deaf Stud Deaf Educ 1998; 3 (2): 135-142. doi: 10.1093/oxfordjournals.deafed.a014343

Celce-Murcia, ., Dörnyei, Z. and Thurrell, S. (1995). "Communicative competence: A pedagogically motivated model with content specifications". *Issues in Applied Linguistics*, 6(2): 5-35.

Cohen, A., & Chi, J.C. (2001). Language strategy use survey. Minneapolis, Minn.: Center for Advanced Research on Language Acquisition, University of Minnesota. Downloadable from the website:
http://www.carla.umn.edu/about/profiles/Cohen

Covey, S. R.; Merrill, A.; Merrill, R. (2017). *First Things First.* New York: Free Press.

Davies, M. (2005). Vocabulary Range and Text Coverage: Insights from the Forthcoming Routledge Frequency Dictionary of Spanish. *Selected Proceedings of the 7th Hispanic Linguistics Symposium,* Cascadilla Proceedings Project, 106-115. Retrieved August 18, 2018, from
http://www.lingref.com/cpp/hls/7/paper1091.pdf

Dixon, S.Y. (2017, July). Creating communities of practice. Keynote address presented at the Teach English Now! Conference, Tempe, AZ.

Dörnyei, Z. & Csizer, K. (1998). Ten commandments for motivating language learners: Results of an empirical study. *Language Teaching Research*, 2(3), 203 – 229.

Dörnyei, Z. (2005). *The psychology of the language learner: Individual differences in second language acquisition.* Mahwah, NJ: L. Erlbaum.

Dunst, C., Meter, D. & Hamby, D. (2011). Influences of sign and oral language interventions on the speech and oral language production of young children with disabilities. Retrieved from http://www.earlyliteracylearning.org/cellreviews/cellreviews_v4_n4.pdf.

Ellis, R. (2008). *The study of second language acquisition.* Oxford: Oxford University Press.

ESPN (2018, August 22). Kobe Bryant on Diana Taurasi's habits and confidence | Musecage | ESPN. Retrieved August 23, 2018, from https://www.youtube.com/watch?v=jALq2vpAKFw

Friedman, A. (2015). America's lacking language skills: Budget cuts, low enrollments, and teacher shortages mean the country is falling behind the rest of the world. *The Atlantic.* Retrieved from https://www.theatlantic.com/education/archive/2015/05/filling-americas-language-education-potholes/392876/.

Fluke, A. (2009, September 2). Bulls chairman Jerry Reinsdorf: Michael Jordan's will to win made him the best. Retrieved from http://www.nba.com/bulls/news/jordanhof_reinsdorf_090902.html/.

Ginseng English (2017, October 24). Most Common English Verb Tenses. Retrieved August 09, 2018, from https://ginsengenglish.com/blog/english-verb-tense-frequency

Gladwell, M. (2008). *Outliers: The story of success*. New York: Little, Brown and Co.

Goodwyn, S., Acredolo, L. & Brown, C.A. (2000). Impact of symbolic gesturing on early language development. Journal of Nonverbal Behavior, 24, 81–103.

Griffiths, C. (2003) Patterns of language learning strategy use. *System*, 31 (3) (2003), pp. 367–383.

Hazenberg, S. & Hulstijn, J.H. (1996). Defining a minimal receptive second language vocabulary for non-native university students: An empirical investigation. *Applied Linguistics* 17,2, 145-163.

Hymes, Dell H. (1972): "On communicative competence". In J. B. Pride and J. Holmes, eds., *Sociolinguistics*. Baltimore: Penguin Books, 269-293.

Klein, K., & Boals, A. (2001). Expressive writing can increase working memory capacity. *Journal of Experimental Psychology: General*, 130, 520 –533.

Jones, R. (2003) "An analysis of lexical text coverage in contemporary German." Presentation given at the Corpus Linguistics 2003 conference, Lancaster University (England), March 2003.

Latham, G. P., & Locke, E. A. (2007). New developments in and directions for goal setting. *European Psychologist*, 12, 290–300.

Lightbrown, P. (1985). Can language acquisition be altered by instruction? in K. Hyltenstam and M. Pienemann (eds.): *Modelling and Assessing Second Language Acquisition*. Clevedon: Multilingual Matters.

Leki, I. (1995). Coping strategies of ESL students in writing tasks across the curriculum. *TESOL Quarterly*, 29, 235

Long, M. (1985). A role for instruction in second language acquisition: Task-based language teaching. In K.
Hylstenstam & M. Pienemann (eds.), *Modelling and Assessing Second Language Acquisition* (pp. 77-99). Clevedon: Multilingual Matters.

Macaro, E. (2006). Strategies for Language Learning and for Language Use: Revising the Theoretical Framework. *The Modern Language Journal*, 90: 320–337.

Mehrabian, A. (1981). Silent messages: Implicit communication of emotions and attitudes (2d ed.). Belmont, Calif.: Wadsworth Pub. Co.

Mueller, P. A., & Oppenheimer, D. M. (2014). The pen is mightier than the keyboard: Advantages of longhand over laptop note taking. *Psychological Science*, 25, 1159-1168.

Norton, B. & K. Toohey (2001). Changing perspectives on good language learners. *TESOL Quarterly* 35.2, 307–322.

Oakley, B. (2013). Learning How to Learn: Powerful mental tools to help you master tough subjects. Retrieved November 17, 2018, from https://www.coursera.org/learn/learning-how-to-learn/

O'Keefe, A., McCarthy, M., & Carter, R. (2017). *From corpus to classroom: Language use and language teaching*. Breinigsville, PA: ICGTesting. Simon & Schuster.

O'Malley, J. M., & Chamot, A. U. (1990). *Learning strategies in second language acquisition*. Cambridge: Cambridge University Press.

Orem, R. (2001). *Journal-writing in adult ESL: improving practice through reflective writing*, in L. English and M. Gillen (eds). Promoting Journal Writing in Adult Education: New Directions for Adult and Continuing Education, no. 90, San Francisco, CA: Jossey-Bass.

Oxford, R. L. (1990). *Language learning strategies: What every teacher should know.* Boston: Heinle & Heinle.

Pienemann, M. (1998). *Language Processing and Second Language Development: Processability Theory.* Amsterdam: John Benjamins. TESOL Quarterly 35.2, 307–322.

Purcell, M. (2016). The Health Benefits of Journaling. Psych Central. Retrieved on July 7, 2017, from https://psychcentral.com/lib/the-health-benefits-of-journaling/

Purpura, J. E. (1999). *Learner strategy use and performance on language tests: A structural equation modeling approach.* Cambridge: Cambridge University Press.

Saragi, T., Nation, P. (1978). *Vocabulary Learning and Reading. System,* 6: 70-78.

Schmidt, R. (1990). The role of consciousness in second language learning. Applied Linguistics 11:17-46.

Trotta, R. (2014). *The edge of the sky: All you need to know about the all-there-is.* Basic Books.

Tugend, A. (2010). The Paralyzing Problem of Too Many Choices. New York Times. https://www.nytimes.com/2010/02/27/your-money/27shortcuts.html

Wesche, M., and Skehan, P. (2002). Communicative teaching, content-based instruction, and task-based learning, In *Handbook of Applied Linguistics*, ed., R. Kaplan, Oxford: Oxford University Press.

Yang, N. (1998). Exploring a new role for teachers: promoting learner autonomy. *System*, 26 (1998) 127-135.

Yule, G, Hoffman, P., and Damico, J. (1987). Paying attention to pronunciation: The role of self-monitoring in perception. *TESOL Quarterly* 21 (4): 765-68.

Made in the USA
San Bernardino, CA
20 December 2018